Python for Data Science:

A Beginners Guide to Learn Data Science Process With Python Programming Language. A Practical Approach to Key Frameworks in Data Science and Machine Learning

Mark J. Branson

Table of Contents

Introduction

Congratulations on the purchase of the book *Python for Data Science* and thank you for doing so.

The following chapters will discuss some of the information that you need to know when it comes to using the Python language to help you handle all of your data science needs. Many companies are spending a lot of time and resources gathering information and data from many different sources. This is a great thing to focus on, but we have to remember that this is not the place to stop. Collecting the data is just one part of the process; we also need to be able to reorganize and then read the information that is inside that data so we can make predictions, come up with better business decisions, and help increase customer satisfaction all in one.

This guidebook is going to take some time exploring all of these parts, and how data science is going to improve so many parts of your business. You may find that this is exactly the process that your company has been trying to get through, and with the help of a good data analysis and some Python coding, you will be able to make all of this happen for you.

This guidebook is going to start out with some information on data science. We will look at the basics that come with data science, how to learn about the ecosystem for data science and to make sure yours is running well with this process, some of the common tasks that data science is able to handle, and even some of the privacy and ethical concerns that come up. We will end this section looking at some of the likely trends and changes that will happen in the future when we talk about data science.

Then we will move on to a few other topics that can help us out with our data analysis and can make the process so much easier. We will look at what machine learning is all about, some of the coding parts that you need to know when you want to learn Python, and some of the best libraries from Python that will allow you to complete any task and create any model that you want to with the help of Python for data science.

The last part of this guidebook is going to give us some practical examples of how we can work with data science, along with some of the coding that makes all of this work. We will look at how to make some data sets, the neural networks, whether they are simple or deep, and even how to work with a dataset that can help filter your emails through as spam or not spam. There is so much that you are able to do with the Python language and data science, and this section is going to take the time to explore all of it.

Python data science is going to make your work so much easier in the long term, and when you can put together all of the different parts that come in this guidebook, you will see that the results you can get are amazing. When you are ready to learn some more about Python for data science and how this coding language, and the process of data science, can really help your business and help you to make smart and data-driven business decisions make sure to check out this guidebook to get started.

There are plenty of books on this subject on the market, thanks again for choosing this one! Every effort was made to ensure it is full of as much useful information as possible, please enjoy!

Part 1:

Getting Started with Data Science

Chapter 1: What is Data Science?

Data science is a process that is going to continue to evolve as one of the most promising, as well as one of the most in-demand career paths for professionals with the right skills to help a business out with this. Today, those professionals in data who are successful understand that they need to advance past some of the traditional skills that were used in the past to go through a lot of data and add in parts like programming skills, and data mining.

In order to uncover some of the useful intelligence that is needed for an organization, the data scientist needs to master the full spectrum of the life cycle of data science, and then gain the right understanding and more to make sure that we are able to maximize the amount of returns that we will get, no matter which phase of the process we are going to be in.

To help us with this though, we need to get a closer look at what data science is going to be all about. Data science is basically going to be the detailed study of how the flow of information, from all of the data that is present in the repository of our organization, can be used. It is going to involve us obtaining any of the meaningful insights that are there from the data that is unstructured and raw, and which we will be able to process through business, programming, and analytical skills.

There is so much that we are able to do with data science and it basically makes life easier for a business. These businesses are already collecting large amounts of data on a regular basis. But even with this large amount of data, they are not going to get ahead until they can really go through that information and find some of the trends and the insights that are there, and then use them in a way to gain an edge over the competition.

In our modern world that is quickly moving moreover to the digital world, many organizations are going to deal with a ton of data, whether it comes in the unstructured or the structured form, each day. Some of the evolving technologies out there have enabled us to find smarter and cost-saving methods to hold and store that data, which makes it even easier than ever for the company to gather a large amount of information and use it for their own needs.

When it comes to where this data is collected from, businesses are going to have a lot of options. And they can collect from a lot of different sources and then see what information is there, or they can choose the ones that they think will hold onto the information that they are looking for. Some of the possible sources that a business may be using in order to gather and collect the data they will use later includes:

1. Some of the sensors that are used in shopping malls that will help to gather information on the shoppers.
2. Posts and comments that are done on social media platforms.
3. Digital pictures and videos that have been captured on our phones.

4. Purchase transactions that have been made through an e-commerce site.

Because of all these sources, it is common for a company to become flooded with all of the data that is presented. Because of all the data that is available, many companies are looking for help to figure out what to do with all of the data, and to learn how they are actually able to take that large amount of data and utilize it for their own needs.

And it is right here where we are going to see some of the concepts that come with data science start to show up in the picture. Data science is able to bring together a ton of skills in one place, including business domain knowledge, mathematics, and statistics in order to help out a business do a number of things. A few of the things that this data is going to be put to use for will include:

1. Reducing the amount of costs that the business has to deal with.

2. Helping to launch a brand new service or product and knowing it will do well.

3. To help gauge the effectiveness that we see in a new marketing campaign.

4. To help tap into some different demographics along the way.

5. To ensure that we can get into a new market and see success.

And these are just a few of the ways that data science is going to come into play and help a business to grow. Any industry, no matter what they sell or who their customers are, will be able to use data science in order to gain success.

Sometimes, it is hard to see how this data science can actually be used. We may think that it is all just a theory, and that there aren't really any businesses out there that use this process for their own needs. However, there are a lot of different companies and industries that are able to use data science for their own needs, including Google, Amazon, and Visa.

Data Science is already taking over the world, and helping out with a lot of different parts like helping the company to reach their customers more efficiently and in the best manner, to help the company to grow, to find new value sources, and more. Let's take a look at how these three big companies are already using data science to help them gain an even bigger competitive edge, so that we can see the results in no time and figure out how these same ideas can be used to benefit our own companies.

To start with is the Visa company. This card company is going to be an online financial gateway for a lot of other companies, meaning that it ends up doing transactions that are worth hundreds of millions each day. Due to the large number of transactions, and all of the money that goes with them, the need for data scientists is big. This company is using the field of data science to help check out for any transactions that are fraudulent, to generate more revenue, and to make sure that the products and services that they are able to offer are customized to each customer.

Amazon is another company that is working with data science to provide a better experience to their customers. Amazon is a name that everyone knows and trusts, and because of this, we know that they are always coming out with new innovations that are meant to help us to enjoy life better and even have fun. Right now this company is working with data scientists to help learn more about the mindset of their customers and to enhance the geographical reach that they have, both with the cloud domain and the e-commerce domain to name a few.

And the final option that we are going to look at is Google. Google is really on a big hiring spree when it comes to looking for trained data scientists. Since most of the products and offerings that Google has are going to be driven by the field of data science, machine learning, and artificial intelligence, they need these kinds of professionals to help out with a bunch of different things all in one.

With that in mind, we need to take a look at what is known as the life cycle of data science. This life cycle is going to help us to know where to find the data we want to work with, how to clean off the data, and how to find the right insights that come with that kind of information as well. Before we go through all of these steps though, we have to come up with a business objective, or a question that we would like to have answered. This is going to help us to focus the research that we do, and can make things a bit easier. With that in mind, it is time to look at what is all a part of the data life cycle and what steps need to be taken to make data science work.

Data Discovery

The first step that comes with the data science life cycle is going to be the process of discovering the data. It is going to be the phase where we discover data from various sources which could be in an unstructured format in some cases, like images and videos. And then we can also go with a format for the data that is more structured, such as a text file. In some cases, it is going to come from more of a relational database system.

Those are some of the traditional forms of collecting data, but it is possible for organizations to explore more and more options as well. For example, there are a lot of companies who are exploring data on customers through social media and more in order to make sure they understand the mindset of their customers better.

Let's say that our objective here is going to be to boost up the sales that we see in our retail store. There are a number of parts that we could consider that are likely to change up the sales and affect the sales that the owner has. Some of the factors that are likely to affect the sales will include:

1. The promotions of the competitor, as well as their physical location.
2. The pricing that you put on the product.
3. The placement of the product.
4. Any promotions that you are running at the time.
5. The working hours when you are open and if they work at the times that is best for your customers.
6. The staff you have

7. The location of your store and whether or not it is easy and convenient for your customers.

When we are able to keep these factors in mind, we would be able to develop clarity on the data that we are discovering, and then we can procure this data to use in the analysis. At the end of this particular stage, we would be able to collect up all of the data that pertains to the elements and factors that we listed above and then it is time to move on.

Preparing the Data

Once we have had a chance to look around and discover the data that we need to help with this process, it is time to prepare the data so that we can actually use it. There are going to be a few things that you can do, but this phase is going to include converting the disparate data into a common format so that all of this is able to work in a seamless manner.

This process is going to involve the data scientist collecting clean data subsets and then inserting the defaults that are right for your needs. In some cases, it is going to involve some methods that are more complex like working to identify some of the values that are missing through modeling, and so much more. Cleaning this data is going to be important, especially if you have to gather the data from more than one source, to ensure that it is going to work the way that you want, that no data is missing, that there are no duplicate values, or anything else that can mess with the model you are making.

Once we are done with cleaning off the data, the next thing that we need to be able to do is integrate and create a good conclusion based on the set of data for an analysis. This analysis is going to involves integrating the data, including merging a few tables together with the same objects but ones that store different information, or summarizing some fields in a table using what is known as aggregation. During all of this, our goal is to explore and then understand the patterns and the values that show up in the set of data that you are working on at the time.

The Mathematical Models

All of the projects that you are going to do with data science are going to come with some mathematical models to help them get done. These models are going to be planned out and then built up by a data scientist in order to help suit the needs that a specific business is going to deal with. The professionals may work with a few different areas that fall into the domain of mathematics including logistics, statistics, differential and integral calculus, and linear regression to name a few.

There are also going to be a few different tools and apparatus to help with this process as well. Some of the R statistical computing tools can help as an advanced analytical tool, Python, SQL, and some of the other visualization tools that are used in this industry.

Also, to make sure that we are coming up with a result that is satisfactory out of all the work you may find that working with just one model on the project is not going to be enough we often need to work with two or more models to get things to work the way that we would like. In this case, the professional is going to work to create a group of models. After measuring out the models, they are going to be able to revise the parameters and then fine-tune them to do the next run of modeling as well. This is a type of process that doesn't take just one round because it can often go through a few of the rounds until the data scientist is sure that they have found the model that works the best for them.

Getting Things in Action

Once we have taken the time to get our data prepared and have built up the models that we would like to use, it is time to get these models to work the right way to get the results that we desire. There could be a few different discrepancies that show up, and a lot of troubleshooting that we have to work with through this process, and this means that the data scientist has to tweak their models a bit, but this is something to be expected and can ensure that in the end, you are going to get a model that works the exact way that you would like.

You have to put the model into work to see how things are going to play out. This is the best way to figure out if the model is actually going to work the way that you would like, or if you need to try out a new algorithm in the process. Or if you need to put more than one algorithm to work at the same time in order to see some good results.

Communication

The next thing that we need to focus on a bit is the idea of communication and how these fit into the data life cycle that we are talking about here. We may forget about this part and how it is going to matter for the data scientist. Without this though, there is going to be some issues with actually being able to use the data and make it work for our needs.

Communicating the things that we have found in the data is the last, but definitely not the least important step when it comes to our endeavors of data science. It is in this stage that the professional is going to be the liaison between the different teams, and they need to be able to communicate in a clear and concise manner the findings that they got out of the other steps. And they have to share this information with a variety of different people including the stakeholders of the company, the big decision-makers of the company, and more.

If the data scientist is not able to explain what they have found in the data, or how they found this information in the first place, there can be troubles. The key people are not going to understand how they should make some of these key decisions, and they may assume that the data analysis is not really worth their time. This is why a data scientist needs to be able to communicate well between all of the different parts of a business.

This communication can be done in a variety of manners. Many times it is going to include the spoken and the written word, but these professionals are going to need to find other ways to work with their communication of the data as well. This can often include some visualization to make things easier and to ensure that the key decision-makers are able to look over the data in a few minutes, rather than having to spend hours going through all of the information.

The data life cycle is so important to helping you to understand what is in all of that data that you have collected over time. Companies are able to collect more data than ever, but they need to know how to take that data and turn it into a form that can actually be used. This is often easier said than done, but by working with the life cycle of data that we talked about before, you will be able to not only collect all of the data, but also put it to good use to make some good business decisions.

Chapter 2: The Ecosystem for Data in Data Science

While the idea of data science isn't something that is brand new, but the demand for data that is quality is something that has exploded recently. This isn't going to be a fad or a type of rebranding, it's more of an evolution. Decisions that are going to govern a lot of the different things that come with a business including how to make the customers happy, what products to sell, and so much more. The neat thing about this though is that all of these decisions are no longer going to be backed by hunches or a guess. Now the decisions are going to be based on real data, data that can provide them with a good action plan along the way.

Because the field of data science is growing at a rapid pace, we now have a big ecosystem of tools that can be used to handle it. Many times there are so many tools to work with that it is hard to know where to start. But learning about the different tools, and some of the ecosystem that comes with the process will ensure that you will see some results as well.

Since data science is something that is cross-functional, many of these companies and tools are going to be hard to categorize. But at the highest level that comes with this, they are going to break down into three main parts of the workflow for the data scientist. What are some of the parts of this workflow? This will include getting ahold of the data, wrangling the data, and then analyzing the data to see what is inside the data.

A data platform is going to seem like something that won' t change on a regular basis, if ever. Many companies had a fixed state of mind when they decided to install their own enterprise database and even their own systems of data warehousing. These were systems that were going to take a very long time to build and then it took even longer to put them in production. Because of this, besides the occasional tune-up or upgrade when it was needed, these data systems were something that needed to last a very long time according to many businesses.

But this is not something that was really seen in this industry. There were a lot of tumultuous changes that were happening in the world of data warehousing analytics and business intelligence, and this ended up pushing the organization to take a new perspective on the platforms that they use for their data. In fact, rather than seeing this as a platform, there are some experts that will use the term of ecosystem in order to describe the emerging data environment.

This is a new term that is going to be an acknowledgment that going into the future, the company is going to focus on the integration and the interdependency of the multiple platforms. This helps to ensure that we are going to use it in the proper manner, and that we will actually be able to see some of the best insights out of that data possible. With this in mind, there are a few trends that we can already look at to see which direction the modern ecosystem of data is likely to head in. The different recommendations that we can follow based on these kinds of trends will include:

Make the Governance of it Your Priority

You will find over time that governance is going to be so important when it comes to the healthy operation of any kind of company that you need to work with. Without this kind of governance, a business is going to risk losing some of the trust that they have in the data, and the resulting analytics. The organization when they are not careful about the governance is often going to be in trouble for some violations of regulations.

As your ecosystem for the data starts to grow some more and adds in more diversity, the governance is something that needs to grow in importance because IT may no longer have a good oversight of the data as they did in the past, and they may not always be able to monitor how it is being used. This is why governance is becoming such a big topic in this kind of industry. Technology solution providers are aware of the interest in governance and are starting to provide better tooling for monitoring data both at rest in databases and in motion across the organization.

The technologies that are used for preparing the data are going to be important when it comes to governing the data, mainly because they are going to help the organization to build up a better knowledge base about the data, how the data can be related even when you use it in more than one source, and how all of this can be moved over to analytics and other parts of your business.

This is also something that comes into place when we are looking at understanding data lineage, which is critical to enabling users to trust their analytics. With the process of data lineage, organizations and companies are going to gain a better understanding of where the data originated from, and they can track how it was changed and transformed as well.

Prepare to Democratize Data Science

Just like some of the other processes in your organization have become more democratized, data science is also something that is going to turn into a more mainstream activity. In the next few years, it is likely that organizations will become less dependent on what are known as unicorns, or those rare individuals who are part data analysts, part programmer, part statistician, and really knowledgeable about what is going on in the world of business. These are hard to find, and only a few businesses who could find one would be able to get ahead and beat out the competition.

Because most organizations are unable to find one of these individuals, much less keep on from moving on to bigger and better things, many of these companies have been assembling teams of data science, where they have an expert in each of these areas individually, but they have all of them work together to get the work of data science down.

Some in this kind of industry do not like the term of citizen data scientist, but it is one of the methods that we are able to use in order to describe a growing constituency of business users who are doing a lot of the work that is needed for a data science project to work. This team is going to be able to build and test all of the models of analytics that they need, perform the statistical analysis, and will employ some of the features of machine learning that are needed for the various tools to work here.

We will also find that organizations have a big need to assemble their ecosystems of data with a good strategy in place, and this strategy needs to support more widespread data science. This process is going to include providing access to data, in data lakes, cloud-based platforms, or in-memory computing that is close to the users, so that many of the users are able to come together, even if they are just an expert in one field, and do some of the activities that come with data science.

Build and Then Share on Customer Intelligence

In all of the various industries that are out today, businesses are going to feel that there is a need to become more focused on the customer than they were in the past. These companies want to be able to preserve and then expand on some of the relationships that they already have with their customers, while attracting some of the best in new customers to keep their company growing. With the help of some of the insights that they are getting from their customers, these companies are working to improve and streamline their operations, while developing services and products that are innovative and will meet the needs of their customers.

This is why it is not all that surprising to see that the latest techniques in machine learning, artificial intelligence, big data analytics, and data visualization are being used in a manner to help improve the intelligence the company has of the customer, and then used to apply that information in the decisions that the company makes.

During this part, companies need to ensure that the ecosystem they are using for the data has the right mix of technologies to help support a continuous pursuit of insights for the customer. Service, sales, and marketing functions are going to be seen as some of the main parts of this, but corporate leadership and product development teams are going to be even more demanding of a lot of knowledge about customer trends. Users will need to tailor their views of this customer intelligence in order to fit it into the context of business and the concept of actionable information as well.

Create an Architecture That is Open, Flexible, and Hybrid

The next thing that we need to take a look at is going to be to create our own architecture. With the warehouses for enterprise data, along with the big data lakes, on-premises systems, and systems that are based on the cloud, historical data and real-time streaming data, it is important for a company to make sure that they don' t pick out a type of architecture that is open and flexible, rather than one that is too rigid.

Business users that are working on these analytics, along with some new applications that are driven by data, are likely to spend their time drawing on several of these sources to satisfy the demands of information. This ends up putting a ton of pressure on data integration and the quality of the master data and the metadata resources. Businesses also need to be able to hold onto the ability to direct workloads to the right platforms, which makes it so that they can take advantage of their respective capabilities.

You do not want the architecture that you want to work with to become this rigid or hard to work with. This makes it really difficult to really handle the data that you have, and can make you miss out on some of the important insights that you need to get out of that data. Being able to keep the architecture as open and broad and as flexible as possible is going to make a big difference when it comes to seeing some great results in the process.

If you are going through all of these, and the idea of these ecosystems seem a bit of daunting, you are not going to be the only one in this industry who feels that way. The platforms, and the monolithic legacy system, are going to seem a lot easier for you to build and then manage. However, even the platform is going to be difficult for us to change when you would like to add in some of the new technologies, or when you would like to be able to make a response to some of the new users that come in, and the demands that you get from these new users as well

This is part of the benefit that comes with using the ecosystem. You are able to move out of some of the rigidity that is present in the system, and instead allow for some more flexibility along the way. Just by the definition of the ecosystem, you will find that it is something that is expected to change and evolve over time, and that is exactly what we are looking for when designing something that works well in data science.

Chapter 3: What You Need to Know About Machine Learning

One topic that we need to spend some time looking at when it comes to data science in the world of machine learning. This is an interesting topic that is going to help us to do a lot of the cleaning of data, and model building, that we need to find the insights that come with all of that data we have created. And it is often easier to work with than we may think. This is even truer when we decide to add in the Python coding language to the mix.

With machine learning, you are teaching the computer or the program to use its own experiences with the user in the past in order to perform better in the future. An example of this would be a program that can help with spam email filtering. There are a few methods that can work in this instance, but the easiest one would be to teach the computer how to categorize, memorize, and then identify all the emails in your inbox that you label as spam when they enter your email. Then, if some new emails come in later that match what is already on your email list, the program would be able to mark these as spam without any work on your part.

While this kind of memorization method is the easiest technique to program and work with, there are still some things that will be lacking with it. First of all, you are missing out on the inductive reasoning in the program, which needs to be there for efficient learning. As a programmer, it is much better to go through and program the computer so that it can learn how to discern the message types that come in and that are spam, rather than trying to get the program to memorize the information.

To keep this process simple, you would program your computer to scan any email that is in the spam folder or already known to be spam. From the scan, your program is going to recognize some phrases and words that appear and are common in these spam messages. The program could then scan through any new emails that you get and if an email matches up quite a bit, then it gets automatically sent to the spam folder.

This is a better method to use. But you do need to watch this one a bit. You must pay attention to what is happening during machine learning and realize that sometimes the program may get it wrong. People would be able to look at these emails and use some common sense to figure out if something is spam or not, but the program can' t do this. This can result in some normal emails going to your spam folder. The programmer would need to be able to catch the mistakes and work to show the computer program how it can avoid these issues later on in the future.

There are a number of benefits that you are going to see when it comes to working with machine learning, especially when it comes to adding this method and the algorithms that go with it. You will find that it can help the machine handle more complex options that it would do on its own. It can handle taking in unknown inputs and then giving the right output that you want. It can speed up the process of completing some complex tasks compared to allowing a human to do the work. And it will be able to get through large sets of data quickly and efficiently, providing you with some of the insights and predictions that you are looking for.

Some of the different benefits that you will be able to see when it comes to applying machine learning, especially when it comes to helping you apply this machine learning to some of the data science that you are trying to focus on will include:

- Statistical research: machine learning is a big part of IT now. You will find that machine learning will help you to go through a lot of complexity when looking through large data patterns. Some of the options that will use statistical research include search engines, credit cards, and filtering spam messages.
- Big data analysis: many companies need to be able to get through a lot of data in a short amount of time. They use this data to recognize how their

customers spend money and even to make decisions and predictions about the future. This used to take a long time to have someone sit through and look at the data, but now machine learning can do the process faster and much more efficiently. Options like election campaigns, medical fields, and retail stores have used machine learning for this purpose.

- Finances: some finance companies have also used machine learning. Stock trading online has seen a rise in the use of machine learning to help make efficient and safe decisions and so much more.

With this in mind, we need to take a look at the three main types of machine learning that can be used. Each of these is going to accomplish slightly different goals when it comes to the work that they can do, and they are going to be trained in a slightly different manner as well. The three types of machine learning that we need to focus on will include supervised machine learning, unsupervised machine learning, and reinforcement machine learning. There are also a number of algorithms that fit into each category, but we are going to focus some time right now on just learning what each of these is all about.

We will take our journey with supervised machine learning to start with. With supervised learning, you are basically teaching the computer the input and the output, so that it knows based on the examples that you have given to it. You will submit both of these together, and the computer or machine is expected to learn what all of these means too.

This method takes longer to do because you have to first send in a lot of training data so that the computer can see as many examples of that as possible. And then you do a testing set to see how successful this process was and how accurate the system can be. The higher quality you can make the examples that you provide, and the more examples with the right answers that you can provide, the higher the accuracy will be when you complete the testing. Remember, as the machine learns more and gets more time with these examples, it will increase its accuracy as well.

Basically, this is like a teacher showing a lot of examples to their students to teach a new lesson. The students will memorize the examples, and from that can remember what examples of a certain lesson are, and can compare this even to values that were not included. They can also figure out from this information what would not fit in with the lesson either, and they get better with the answers as time goes on. The computer system is going to do the same thing when it comes to supervised machine learning, but it does it on a much bigger scale as well.

Now that we know a bit more about the supervised machine learning, it is time for us to explore a bit more about how unsupervised machine learning is going to work. Supervised machine learning is going to rely on a lot of data and examples that will be fed into the machine for the training period, and then a lot of this data can be used to help test it out and see how much information was retained. This is a lot of work for the programmer because they have to sort out the data into the two sets, and they have to do all of the work here.

Another option to work with though is known as unsupervised machine learning. This method is going to help a computer or a machine learn the right way that you would like it to behave without showing it a ton of examples to start out with. Unsupervised machine learning is going to be the type of model that is used that can take the algorithm and learn from its mistakes or from examples, without needing to have an associated response to go along with it. This shows us how these algorithms are going to be in charge of analyzing and figuring out all of the data patterns that are present, based on the input that you provide, without the given output in place.

Now, there are a few choices that we can work with here to make sure that we get the system to work while using unsupervised machine learning. No matter which of these algorithms you are choosing to use with these, it is able to take all of the data that you present to it, and then restructure it in a manner so that the data can fall into some classes that make sense.

This is going to be a process that makes life easier for the programmer to take a look at the data when it makes sense for them. This kind of learning is a good one to bring out for a lot of the data analysis that you want to use because it can set up the computer to handle a lot of the work, and you don' t have to be right on top of it, writing out a lot of code or having to present many different examples to the algorithm to make it work.

One example of this that you can consider is going to be if you are in a business that would like to take all of the data that you are working with, and then read through it all, using that information to make predictions. Another example is how search engines are going to run on some of the algorithms that come with machine learning.

Reinforcement machine learning is going to be the third option when it comes to using machine learning. This one is going to be a little bit different compared to what we will see with the other two sets of algorithms, but it helps us to train our machines in a slightly different manner than before. We can remember that this is going to rely mostly on the idea of true and false to provide us with the answers that we want.

There are some people who see reinforcement learning as the same thing as unsupervised learning because they are so similar, but it is important to understand that they are different. First, the input that is given to these algorithms will need to have some mechanisms for feedback. You can set these up to be either negative or positive based on the algorithm that you decide to write out.

So, whenever you decide to work with reinforcement machine learning, you are working with an option that is like trial and error. Think about when you are working with a younger child. When they do some action that you don' t approve of, you will start by telling them to stop or you may put them in time out or do some other action to let them know that what they did is not fine. But, if that same child does something that you see as good, you will praise them and give them a ton of positive reinforcement. Through these steps, the child is learning what acceptable behavior is and what isn' t.

To keep it simple, this is what reinforcement machine learning is going to be like. It works on the idea of trial and error and it requires that the application uses an algorithm that helps it to make decisions. It is a good one to go with any time that you are working with an algorithm that should make these decisions without any mistakes and with a good outcome. Of course, it is going to take some time for your program to learn what it should do. But you can add this into the specific code that you are writing so that your computer program leans how you want it to behave.

All three of these methods for machine learning are going to be important when it comes to getting things to work in data science. Often the method that you go with, and the algorithms that make the most sense for you will depend on the data you want to go through, and the types of insights you would like to get out of that data as well. Sometimes your end goal with the data is going to make a difference as well.

Machine learning is definitely something that is going to provide you with a lot of good results when working in data science. In the data science life cycle that we talked about before, when you are ready to form your own model and receive the right insights and more, you would often use some of the algorithms that come with machine learning to put it all together. Learning the three types of algorithms, and how machine learning can come into play here will make data science so much easier to work with.

Chapter 4: Common Tasks for Data Science

There are a lot of different tasks that you can use data science to help out with. It is helpful for sorting through all of the data that you have been collecting over the past time, and it can help you to make predictions, choose which products you would like to release to the market, and even make predictions about how the economy will behave in the future. All of this comes together to help see why companies all over are deciding to work with data science and some of the different methods that come with them. Some of the common tasks that you can do with the help of data science will include:

Can Sort Through Large Amounts of Data?

The number one reason that companies like to work with data science is because it helps them to get through a large amount of data. It is pretty much considered a common business practice to gather up a lot of data, and this information is going to come to us in a variety of formats as well. This means that we need to be prepared to handle the data, and actually learn what is inside of all this data.

Companies are going to gather all of this data from a large variety of sources. You can get this data from your social media account, from asking questions, from doing research studies, from taking research that others have done, and more. While collecting this data is a very important part of the data science process, it is still important for us to be able to go through and actually gather legitimate information that can help us to learn some important insights and make predictions about the future.

In the past, companies did not gather as much information about the industry and about their customers. These companies were also a lot smaller and often had less competition so this kind of thing was not necessary. But in our modern world, collecting the data and then using it properly is one of the only ways that you can keep up, and hopefully surpass, the other companies in your industry.

While many companies wonder if it is worth their time to hire a data scientist to do all of the algorithms and work, think about how long it would take for someone to manually sift through all of that information? With the algorithms and the ideas with data science, you will be able to go through all of the information in a short period of time, and glean out all of the information that is needed

Can Help Companies Make Predictions?

Being able to predict the future is one of the best ways to be prepared for what is coming, and to keep your business up and running whether times are good, or times are bad. The data that you are able to collect from doing data science, and the insights that you receive from the right algorithm are going to go far in helping your company predict what is going to happen in the future, and can make it easier to still make money, no matter how the economy is doing.

Let's say that it is going to be a cold winter, unusually cold and you would like to know how that is going to affect your sales for this season. You take a look at the sales, and notice that on the other cold winters like this one, the sales for your product actually went up. Maybe you sell video games and more people purchase these because they are stuck inside and it is too cold to do some of the typical outdoor activities.

With this in mind, and with checking several models to make sure that the weather is predicted to act in this manner, you can plan out how you will handle the winter. Maybe you keep some extra stock on hand to handle the influx of customers. You can consider extending your hours more than usual to catch these people as they get off work. Keeping enough staff on hand to ring customers up and to answer questions, stock, and do other things to run your business can help as well.

But say that it is going to be a warm winter, and this usually means that your sales go down. After verifying the information, you may decide to cut back on hours, and not hire anyone new for the season when some of your summer works head off to school or somewhere else. You may keep a more limited stock and just special order if someone wants a game or another product that you do not have on the floor.

In both of these cases, you are able to gather in lots of information about the upcoming weather, as well as information about how you and others in the industry have seen sales. And then you can make the right predictions on how you should stock things, how many employees should be on staff, and more to keep things organized, to maximize your profits no matter the season, and to ensure you keep your customers happy and satisfied in the process.

Can Help Companies Decide Which Products to Produce?

Depending on how you choose to use the data you have, it is possible to use data science to help determine which products you should produce. Many businesses who are embracing data science will use this to figure out what products they should offer to the market next. While this process may take a bit longer since you need to collect all of the data and sort through it over time, it ensures that the product is going to be more accepted by the market, and that you will actually make a profit, rather than just making any product you choose without the research behind it.

Think about how much risk there used to be when creating and marketing a product. You may know the business world a bit, and sometimes there are some ideas that you just know will be big hits. But there is always some risk if you don' t include the market opinion and your customers in the decision. You could spend months and even years working on a new product and developing it, and then find out that it is not something that does well. Even if it does well but misses your targets, this could be a big loss of money and time, and many businesses have gone under from something like this.

But when we use data science, we can take some of the risk out of it. You have to make sure you are gathering the information from the right place, and you can' t just make any assumptions that you want along the way, but if you use the process of data science properly, you could have data behind your decisions, ensuring that the risk you take on is limited, and that you will see the best results in the process. There is no guarantee that there will be no risk, but with data science, you take that very high risk and move it down to a minimum.

Can Improve Customer Satisfaction?

Many companies have found that working with data science is one of the best ways that they can increase the amount of customer satisfaction they are dealing with. And in our modern world, we need to always make sure that the customer is the primary focus and that we are providing the customer with what they really want. There are a lot of companies out there, and many are selling the same or a similar product. What really differentiates a company and helps them to grow is how they treat their customers, and what they can do to increase customer satisfaction in the process.

There are a lot of different methods that you can use in order to learn more about your customer, and what they are really looking for when they use your business. You can use surveys to ask them about their experience if they have shopped with you before, or even a survey of potential customers to see what would bring them to your store in the first place. Social media is another place where a lot of marketers are turning to gain more insights about their customers.

All of this information can be brought together to help a company learn who their customers are, how to provide a better product or service, and how they can make the customer happy. Often new product ideas are found here, and sometimes this is a place where we really should take a look at the outliers in our information, but this can open up an exciting new market or product for you to try out before the competition.

Can help the company save money

Many times companies are going to work with data science because it is an easy way for them to learn where they can effectively cut costs and improve their bottom line. Every business wants to be able to save money where they can, and increase their bottom line, but sometimes without the insights that data science can provide, this is hard to even get started with.

When we talk about cutting down on costs though, our goal is not to cut down and make a cheaper product or cut corners and make something that no one wants to buy or something that is not safe to work with. Our goal with this one instead is more about finding the places where waste is going on, and we're improving that area will not cause any negative effects on the product or service. In fact, often we are able to improve the product or service when we do take steps to reduce the waste.

For example, we may use data science to figure out where the lulls in production are and then figure out ways to reduce how long these lulls are. Data science and data analysis have been done to figure out when a machine will need an upgrade or a new part, and then these are scheduled at night or other downtimes to reduce the amount of time that is wasted repairing the item during normal working hours. Sometimes the data science can be done to learn better ways of production, how to shorten the assembly line and save time, while making the job easier for the employees, and so much more.

You may be surprised at how many different ways data science can help your business to save money, and this has nothing to do with cutting corners or doing something that is likely to drive your customers away. This makes it the perfect solution for many businesses who want to increase their bottom line, while still beating out the competition with high-quality products their customers are going to love.

Data science is able to come on board and help out with many different processes along the way. You will find that when this all comes together, it is going to do nothing but improve your business, as long as you are able to follow the insights that are found in the data you collect. Sometimes you gather up the data with a specific goal or question in mind, and other times you may decide to just look through the data and see what predictions it can make for you. When all of this comes together though, you are going to be amazed at what data science can do for you.

Chapter 5: Privacy and Ethical Concerns

One topic that has concerned a lot of people when it comes to data science is how we are going to protect the privacy of others, and how are we going to maintain the ethics that are needed in all the different industries. Companies want to be able to collect this data, and then learn from it as much as possible. But when they use the wrong practices, and they are not careful about who gets ahold of some of the information, then many privacy and ethical concerns are going to start showing up.

With all of the advances that are taking over with data science, and with this technology creating more tools for automated decision making, how are businesses across many industries going to handle some of the potential problems that can come up. Those who work in this kind of field, along with the field of analytics, are going to be right at the front of this digital transformation, and opportunities for achieving social good within this kind of field are going to be huge. In just a few short years, we have already seen how data has become one of the most valuable commodities when we look at the global economy.

The vast quantities of data that we can get from users of social media, from apps, and from devices on IoT have created a ton of information that businesses are more than happy to get their hands on. This is because the companies are able to take all of this information and mine out vital insights on how to solve problems, help out the customer, and gain a competitive edge.

Of course, this can go one of two ways. The information that is presented can be used in order to help the business thrive and to ensure the world is a better place. Or the information can be used in a bad way, or an unethical manner that only ends up benefiting the person who gathers the information, and perhaps harming others.

The way that this data is going to head will hinge on the continuing development of a framework that is ethical, an increased amount of transparency with the public about the use of the data, and a constant cognizance of potential biases, both within the set of data you are using, and the human who is doing the work, that could be used when you do decision making that is automated, or any other advances in technology.

Today, the field of big data is going to give us unprecedented insights and opportunities across all of the different industries that use it, from the financial world to manufacturing and even to healthcare to name a few. But it is also going to raise some concerns and questions that anyone who wants to use this in an ethical manner needs to address.

The relentless changes that are happening to technology on a daily basis, and all of the many sources of Big Data are already keeping professionals in this industry on their toes and the reality is that the organizations that use Big Data, and the tech departments, agencies from the government, consumers, and even protection groups for consumers are all having trouble keeping up.

With this in mind, we need to make sure that we are paying attention to some of the concerns that come with privacy and other ethical things with this Big data. Namely, there are going to be three concerns that come with big data that are the most worrisome, and that we need to make sure to regulate and watch out for while ensuring that the personal information of the customer is in mind, and allowing these companies to gather the data. These three issues are going to include data discrimination, data security, and data privacy. Let's take a closer look at each one to get a better idea of how they work together, and what we need to consider on each one as we work through data science.

Data Privacy

The first thing that we need to be concerned about is data privacy. In 1791, the 4th Amendment was ratified, and it was set up to give citizens in the United States a reasonable expectation of privacy. Of course, when this was created and added to our Constitution, there was no way for our Founding Fathers to even dream about all of the different complications from 21st-century technology and how we would need to be able to manage all of these at some point.

There is no doubt that we are going to benefit from a lot of the breakthroughs and conveniences that come with apps and services that have been powered by big data. Many times we enjoy these on a regular basis and may use them in our daily lives. But even with the benefits that come with these devices and even despite the way they make life better, we also have to consider what kind of risk is happening to our privacy? Do we even get to have any control of how much, and what type, of our personal information is being used in these cases?

Right now in the world of technology, we are at a point where even if we went on a total boycott of technology, it may not be enough to protect us all of the way. This is, of course, you plan to just walk to all of the locations you want to go, you wear a mask all of the time so that facial recognition technology won't see you, and you use cash that has never been deposited into a financial institution.

Succeeding at getting through our modern world without any kind of technology, and much of that technology is already being run by machine learning, can be tricky, and it isn't going to be a guarantee that you will protect the privacy all of the time. But it does show us exactly how prevalent big data and data science has become, and how much of the simple pieces of technology that we use on a daily basis are already relying on machine learning and other important parts of this process.

It is true that much of the information that is being collected in these scenarios is going to be used in a manner that is more benign, but the potential for this data, data that is more sensitive in nature, to be used for evil can be a real possibility at some point. And because of this, the U.S. government is still trying to determine the best method to use to help with regulating the internet privacy rules for example. Congress is currently in a debate to adopt rules that would require internet service providers to tell their customers when information is collected, what type of information is collected, and how this information can be used and shared.

While the outcome of this legislation is still in the air, American lawmakers may want to work with some of the ideas that were introduced by the European Union and focus on creating a nice environment that is able to protect their people. For example, the EU' s General Data Protection Regulation is going to be implemented with a big goal of giving citizens their control back over personal data. This is going to be a regulation that will apply to any kind of company that is holding data about any of the citizens in the European Union, whether the company is originally stationed there or someone else.

While there are some government interventions that are happening to keep this data in check and make sure that companies are using all of that data in an ethical manner, we always have to remember that ethical business practices, even when it comes to the data that you are collecting, is just good business. It is always best for a company to work with more transparency than not, and ethically using data is so important. Not because it is the right thing to do, though this is important with data, but because there are more regulations coming, and because it keeps an open and trusting relationship going between you and the customers.

Data Security

The next thing that we need to take a look at is going to be data security. So, your customer went through your website and clicked and agreed to having their data used, and analyzed, by your company. This is often done because the customer feels that they are going to be able to benefit from the service and the product, and they decide that these benefits will far outweigh the loss of privacy that is going to happen. But with this in mind, is the customer really able to trust that your company will work to keep all of that data safe and secure? This is a question that is becoming harder for any business, even good and reputable businesses, to answer all of the time.

As big data continues to grow in size, and the web of connected devices keeps ongoing, it is going to expose even more of our data to potential breaches in security. We have already seen that there are many different organizations that are struggling to handle the security of their data, and this is before they added in some of the complexities that happen when they use big data. And once that big data is added to the process, many of them start to feel like they are drowning to keep up.

First, these companies are playing a bit of catch up and trying to close the gap that is coming in with their big data skills. This is mostly due to the fact that there are just too few data security professionals with expertise to feel confident that all business has a handle on the security of the data they collect. Some companies can afford to have a good team like this. But right now, there are just not enough professionals to go around, and this means that some companies, no matter how hard they try, may not have the right team in place to ensure the data stays safe.

The biggest solution that is going to come in here when it comes to the security of the information that is saved could reside in a Big data-style analysis. With this method, threats can be detected, and in some cases prevented, simply by doing the process that we have already talked about in this guidebook. You just need to analyze the data.

Data Discrimination

When everything else is known about the person, is it going to become acceptable to discriminate against people based on the data that we already have on their lives? We already use credit scoring in the financial world to help determine who is going to be allowed to borrow money, and most of the things that come with insurance will be driven by data. While big data is set up as a way to help businesses provide better services while marketing better at the same time, because they have all of this data, it is going to make it easier for them to discriminate as well.

There is a general acceptance right now by most consumers that they are already being analyzed and assessed in greater detail, and the result of this analysis is going to be a better experience. But, what if all of this new insight is going to actually turn things around and make it more difficult for certain people to get the resources or the information that they need? This has already become a concern and is something that many industries and businesses are looking into to try and prevent.

There are already a lot of consumer protection laws in place to help with this. For example, the Federal Trade Commission Act and the Fair Credit Reporting Act are all going to be laws put in place that are applicable to an analysis done by Big Data. Companies have to follow these acts, along with any of the laws for equal opportunity, in mind to make sure they are following all of the rules and being fair and ethical in the process.

In addition to making sure that all of the regulations for that industry are taken care of, and that your customers are treated in the best and more fair method possible, there are a few other steps that a company who wants to utilize big data can keep in mind. Companies need to check all of the data to ensure the following:

1. The data is going to actually be a representative sample of the consumers of their products.
2. That the algorithms are not only set up to work, but that they will prioritize fairness.
3. That the company has a good awareness of the biases that can show up in the data.
4. That these companies are already checking their big data outcomes against some of the traditionally applied statistics processes.

As Big data continues to evolve over time, and companies find new ways to use it, and even to gather the information that they use, these three concerns that we talked about above, are going to be priority items to work with. Everyone needs to be concerned with these to ensure that not only can these companies gather the information that they need to make some smart decisions, but that the customer is going to be able to maintain their privacy and see some good results in the process.

Chapter 6: The Future Trends to Watch Out For When It Comes to Data Science

One of the best things to watch out for when it comes to working in data science is imagining where this is going to take us in the future. There is already so much that we are able to do when it comes to data science, artificial intelligence, and even machine learning, and it is always fun to imagine where this is all going to take us in the next ten, twenty, and even thirty years from now. With that in mind, let's dive into some of the future trends that we should watch out for when it comes to where data science is going to take us in the future.

Regulatory Schemes

The first thing that we are going to look at when it comes to the future of data science is regulatory schemes. With all of this data that is being generated every second of every day, and the pace accelerating all of the time thanks to options like IoT, the issue of data security that we talked about earlier is going to become more important, rather than less important, as time goes on. This means that companies need to step up their game and find new ways to not only collect the data, but to make sure that any data they collect stays secure and safe for their customers.

It is reasonable to expect that in the years to come, there is going to be more data regulations that show up. Data regulatory events, like the European General Data Protection Regulation from 2018 that we talked about helped to regulate the data science practice that most companies were performing by setting up certain boundaries and limits on the management, as well as the collecting of personal data.

These regulatory activities are going to be important because they ensure that the company is going to act not only in their best interests, but also in the best interests of their customers, and can help to protect valuable and personal information in the process. These regulatory activities, while positive, are going to really impact some of the predictive models that are used in the future, along with a few of the analytic exercises that companies like to employ on the data they collect.

Artificial Intelligence and Some Intelligent Apps

Artificial intelligence is definitely a buzz word that is flowing around the business world right now, especially where it relates to data science and machine learning. Being able to train a machine or a system how to behave on its own, without a lot of human interaction or someone going in and coding each and every step of the process, is a really unique thing that we can do, and many companies are jumping on board in no time.

It is unlikely that all of this commotion that has shown up around artificial intelligence will die down in the next few years. Instead, more and more companies are likely to jump on board with this and see some of the amazing things that artificial intelligence is able to help out with. As time goes on, we are likely to see more advanced applications of this artificial intelligence, no matter what field or industry is using it.

Right now, we see that harnessing all of the power that comes with artificial intelligence is still a big challenge and we will likely need to work with it more to see some improvements. More intelligent apps are going to be developed in the future using AI, machine learning, and other similar pieces of technology as well. Another thing that we can watch out for in the future is automated machine learning because it is able to transform what we do with data science in a much better manner that we can do with data management.

Over time, it is believed that we are going to see a development of specific hardware that can be used for the training and the execution of deep learning, which is such an important part of all of this. The incorporation of artificial intelligence over time is going to help enhance the kinds of decisions that all companies make, while enhancing the experience that is there for everyone. It is likely that where it relates to data science and the process we have discussed in this guidebook, applications and services are going to rely on artificial intelligence more and more in order to improve how well they are able to function.

What this means is that the market is going to see a huge rise in the next few years when it comes to how many intelligent apps are going to be used. Intelligent things are basically just the smarter version, or the version that is run by artificial intelligence, of regular gadgets. These will flood the market, improving the bottom line for many companies, and the lifestyle of most of their customers.

Virtual Representations Of Objects in the Real World, and Real-Time Innovations

Another thing that is likely to become more widespread over the next few years in the world of data science is going to be the idea of digital representations of physical objects that we see in real life, and these objects are going to be powered by the capabilities that come with artificial intelligence. These technologies are going to be used by businesses all over in order to help them solve real-life business problems, no matter where that company is located throughout the world.

The pace of real-time innovations may have been something that seemed impossible in the past, but it is definitely something that we can focus on now, and you will find that these kinds of innovations are going to accelerate with some of the more advanced technologies that are likely to come out over the next few years as well.

Machine learning and neural networks are going to be used to help out with these applications, and new algorithms may be developed to help handle all of this. Both applications of virtual reality and augmented reality are already giving way to some big transformations in this kind of field. It is likely that there will be more breakthroughs in these areas, and in more, in the next year, and it is believed that the machine to human interaction is going to improve because of all these factors coming together. Of course, we will also see a rise in the experiences and expectations of humans when it comes to these digital machines and systems they are using.

Edge Computing

It is expected that the world of I1T is likely to continue growing, and as a result, edge computing is going to become more and more popular as the years go on. With all of the thousands of devices, and even sensors, working to collect as much data as possible to be analyzed, businesses are finding that it is worth their time to do more of their data processing and their analysis closer to the source of origin for this data. This is going to change up the way that data is consumed in many manners, and can make it so that the way the data is collected, and the type of data that is taken in, will be different in a few years compared to what it is today.

In this process, we are likely to see hat edge computing is going to be on the rise to make sure that we can maintain a close proximity to the source of the information. The closer the business can be to the source of the information, the more accurate the information is, the more information they can get, and the sooner they can get their hands on that information as well.

Issues related to latency, connectivity, and bandwidth is also going to be solved through this. Edge computing, along with some of the cloud technology that is so prevalent with data science, will provide us with a coordinated structure that will simulate a paradigm of the service-oriented model. In fact, one prediction that is done by IDC already predicts the following, "By 202, new cloud pricing models will service specific analytics workloads, contributing to 5X higher spending growth on cloud vs. on-premises analytics." Think about how much power that one thing has, and it is likely to take over and cause a stir in the world of data science in no time at all.

Blockchain

If you have spent any time paying attention to the world of cryptocurrencies like Blockchain and Ethereum, then you have a good idea of what the blockchain is all about.

It is definitely a unique piece of technology that we are not going to delve into too deeply in this guidebook, but it is still something that is good to know about and use for our benefits here.

Blockchain is a major piece of technology that is going to underlie a lot of the most popular cryptocurrencies out there, including Bitcoin. To keep this simple, the Blockchain is going to be a highly secure ledger that helps to run these currencies, and there are actually a number of different applications that can be used along with it. For example, if we can make some small modifications when it comes to this technology, it is possible to use it to record a huge number of transactions with a surprising amount of detail.

If we add in some data science and some of the various machine learning algorithms that we have already discussed in this guidebook, we can see how it will combine with the blockchain technology to have some far-reaching implications, especially when it comes to data security. It is likely that some of the changes that we will see when it comes to the future of data science will include some new measures of security and the process of emulating the blockchain technology.

With these trends likely to show up in the next year or so, the future for business and innovation working hand in hand looks pretty bright. Like big data, the world of data science is going to witness a lot more use, and a lot of development in the next few years, and where this kind of information and technology is going to take us is still unknown. Before we know it, both the physical world and the digital world will become increasingly more intertwined until we are hardly able to tell them apart.

For example, it won' t be long before some of the experiences that we can have in the digital world will get more incorporated in the experiences that we have on a daily basis. With the trends that we have listed above expected to persist, plus a lot of other innovations that are likely to come out in the near future, the field of data science are expected to see some more development and exposure beyond measure.

Chapter 7: An Introduction into the World of Python

Now that we have had a chance to work with the idea of data science and all of the different parts that we need to know when it comes to data science and how to do a proper analysis, it is time for us to look a bit at some of the programming that we are able to use here. There are actually quite a few different coding languages that we are able to use that can make data science, and data analysis with, but one of the best, and the easiest to learn, is going to be the Python coding language.

There are a lot of benefits that come with using the Python coding language, rather than some of the other coding languages out there. Some programmers are a bit worried about introducing this coding language into machine learning and data science because they think it is too easy and too simple to work with these two topics. But while Python is designed to work well with beginners who are just entering into the world of coding, it does have enough power to help us get all of these tasks done.

Python is a great coding language to work with, and as you go through some of the more advanced of the algorithms that go along with machine learning, as well as neural networks that can be created in this guidebook, you will find that even these complicated things are easy to read through and understand.

And that is part of the beauty that comes with using the Python coding language. It is simple to use and understand. It has been designed knowing that the end-user is often going to be a beginner, someone who hasn' t had a lot of experience with the whole coding thing at all, but who is still interested in being able to explore how to code and all of the things that machine learning is able to help out with.

There are a lot of things that you will enjoy when it comes to using the Python language. As we have already been able to discuss a bit, you will enjoy that it is designed with the beginner in mind. This makes it easier to use and ensures that even if you have not been able to work with coding in the past, you will still have a chance to learn and write some of your own codes. While we aren't going to have time to talk about coding in Python here, all of the codes that we have for deep learning later in this guidebook are written with the help of the Python language.

Even though this particular language is easy to learn and even easy to read, there is a ton of power that comes with this kind of coding language. Some more advanced programmers who will even be able to use this coding language because it allows them to have the freedom to work on really complex things, like machine learning, without having to worry about some of the complications that happen with other coding languages.

As a beginner, you are going to appreciate that there is a large community to work with when it comes to Python. There are many different programmers from beginners to advanced who use this coding language, and they all come together on various forums and communities. You can easily use these to your advantage to learn how to code in this language, and how to get the results that you are looking for, even when you get stuck.

As we will explore in the next chapter, the extensions that come with the Python coding language are going to be pretty neat as well. While the regular library that comes with Python is going to be a good one to learn some of the language and can help you to get some of the basics of coding done. But if you want to do some of the more complex things that are needed in data science and with machine learning, you will need to add in some of these extensions to help you get the work done the right way.

As you can already see here, there are a lot of beneficial parts that come with working on the Python language, and this can be the key that you need to finally get your coding all done. Let's take a look at some of the benefits that come with the Python language, as well as some of the most basic parts that are present in this language to learn exactly how we can make this language our own with data science.

The Benefits of Python

There are a lot of choices out there that you can make when it comes to working on data science, or even just learning a language on its own. You can choose to work with languages that are best for writing websites, some that work with one operating system over another, and some that are going to work best for databases and more.

You will find though that one of the best coding languages that you are able to learn, the one that will ensure that you really see some results, while being easy enough for a beginner to learn how to use, is the Python coding language. It works well on simple coding processes, but also can come into play with data science, deep learning, artificial intelligence, and machine learning. Some of the great benefits that you will be able to see when it comes to working with the Python language, no matter what your goal is for your coding project, will include:

The Python coding language is easy to read, being done in English, and the work that you need to do is going to be kept to a minimum. There are no extra lines that are not necessary, and even as you read through some of the different options that we talk about in this guidebook, and some of the examples that we provide, you will find that it is easy to read through them, even before you get started and even know what they mean.

As we are talking about this though, you may be a bit nervous about using the language. Maybe it seems a bit strange that you would need to use a language that is designed for beginners to help do things like machine learning and more complicated tasks. But you will find that this language, even though it is maybe easier than some of the other languages out there, and designed with the beginner in mind, is meant to have a lot of power as well. As we go through some of the libraries below that work well with machine learning and artificial intelligence,

Python is still the perfect language to help you get all of these algorithms and tasks that you want to do.

This is just the start of some of the benefits that you are going to enjoy when you decide to work with the Python coding language. Another benefit is all of the different libraries that come with this language as well. The basic library of Python is going to be pretty simple to work with, and can add in a lot of the functionality that you need with coding. This is great news, but you can take this a bit further and watch how adding some of the extensions and other libraries that are available with Python are going to increase what you can do as well. This can help with things like machine learning, mathematical equations, science, engineering, and more than the traditional library of Python may not be able to handle on its own.

Another benefit that a lot of beginners like about this language is that it has a large community. This is going to be beneficial because you can easily find those who are willing to answer your questions, show you examples, and ensure that you are able to see some good results when it comes to any problems with your coding. Since so many people throughout the world are already relying on this coding language, and have learned how to use it, you will find that it is very easy to get help when things get tough, or when you are looking for new ways to do some of your coding.

Python is also going to be an easy code to test out. You want to make sure, especially when it comes to data science and machine learning, to make sure that you are able to test the code that you are trying to write out. This ensures that you are not just writing code that is going to be full of lots of errors, but that the code is going to work the way that you want along the way.

There are a lot of methods that you are able to use when it comes to testing out the code you would like to write, and testing it out early on and often will ensure that you are able to get the results that you want out of the code, without being worried that it won' t work later on. Rather than worrying about having things get messed up with the test, or deciding that you shouldn' t have to work with the testing at all because it seems too complicated in the first place, the testing that is done with Python is going to be easier, which provides any kind of programmer with the peace of mind they need to get the program done and working right.

It works well with machine learning. And the number one biggest benefit that comes with working on Python is that it is going to work well with machine learning. There are a lot of different parts of machine learning, and often you can choose to go with another kind of coding language if you would like. But when it comes to power and ease of use, and the different libraries that work specifically well with machine learning like Python does. These are just a few of the reasons why Python is going to work so well with artificial intelligence and machine learning as well.

As you can see here, there are a lot of different benefits that come with working on Python machine learning, and Python can really be a great language that you should spend your time learning about and understanding. It is simple with a lot of power, has all of the extensions and capabilities that you are looking for when working on a programming language, and can help you to handle any of the machine learning algorithms and tasks that you would like to get done. And that is why we are going to spend more time in the rest of this guidebook exploring all of the libraries and methods that you can use to make Python work with machine learning.

The Basic Parts of Python

There are a lot of different parts that come with working on the Python language. Knowing some of the basics that come with this coding language, and the different ways that we can use these even in some more complicated types of codes can be very important. As a beginner who wants to be able to use the Python code to help out with data science, it is a good idea to learn a bit about these different types of codes that come with Python. Some of the basics that come with this language that we need to focus on will include:

1. The keywords

It is important to know a bit more about the keywords that come with this language. These keywords are going to be responsible for telling the compiler for Python how to act. Without one of these keywords in place, the compiler is going to have no idea of what it needs to do. And if you put one of the keywords in the wrong location, you are going to end up with an error message because the compiler still is not sure what actions you would like it to use. Learning more about these keywords and how you can use them for your needs will make a big difference in how well your codes work for you.

2. The identifiers

The second item that we need to be able to explore when it comes to some of the basics of the Python code is the identifiers. There are a lot of different types of identifiers that we are able to work on, and they are helpful in getting the code to behave the way that you want. Each of the various identifiers is going to come with a different name including the functions, variables, and classes.

We need to focus on the right way that we can name these identifiers to make sure that they call up the right part of the code. Even though there are different types of identifiers, you will be able to use the same rules in naming them to get some of the best results. However, we need to make sure that we use the right rules when writing out the identifiers or the code is not going to know the right parts that should be pulled up when the code is running.

So, to help us make sure that we are naming the identifiers in the right manner, the first rule that we need to keep in mind is picking out which name we want to work with. The neat thing here is that there are a lot of examples and you do have quite a bit of freedom on what you are doing with these. You can use any kind of letter, both the uppercase and the lowercase letters, the numbers, and even the underscore symbol to get the work done. Any combination of those options is going to be fine for the name as well.

However, you have to remember that there is an order that needs to happen with these, or they are not going to react the way that you would like. First, you are not able to start the name of this identifier with a number. You also do not want to leave any spaces if you are using more than one word to name the identifier. So, you are not able to write out the name of an identifier as "3 kids" or "three kids" but you could do "three kids" or "three kids" and it would save right. If you try to go against any of these rules, you will see that the compiler will bring up an error signal for you.

When you are trying to pick out the name that you would like to give your identifier, you can easily pick from the rules above and also remember that you need to pick out a name that you will be able to remember and that makes sense for that part of the code. If you are writing out the code and you named an identifier something that you are not able to remember, or something that is difficult, then you will run into trouble adding it in later on. But outside of those few rules, you are able to give your identifier any name that you would like.

3. **Looking at the statements**

This one is pretty simple, but we are going to take a quick look at these so we know what these are all about when you hear about them in your coding. When we bring up the statements in Python, we are just talking about a string of words in the code that the program or the compiler will be able to write up for us, and will show up on the computer screen for you. If you want the code to write up something like "Hi, welcome to Python" the part in the quotes would be the statement in this code.

4. The comments

No discussion on the Python code, or any other kind of coding language that you would like to work with. These comments are going to be a great way that you are able to add in some little notes, or even naming a part of the code, to make it easier to read. You will be able to add in these simple comments to any part of the code that you would like, and the compiler will know that it should just skip over this part and move on.

To work with the comments, you just need to add in the # symbol. Then you can write down all of the information that you would like without ruining any of the code that is around it. The compiler is going to see the # symbol, and then will just skip over that part and move on to the next piece of code. You can add in as many of these kinds of comments as you would like to help explain the different parts of the code, but it is often best if you can keep the number of comments to a minimum. This helps to make the code easier to read, and ensures that the most important parts are going to be the main focus here.

5. The variables

Another topic that we need to take a look at is going to be the variables. These variables are important when it comes to coding in Python because they show up often in the various codes that you are writing. The variables are going to be present because they will store some of the values that you would like to add from the code into the memory that you have. and when you work to assign a value over to one of the variables, it ensures that all of the parts are going to stay in place and look nice.

One thing that you will notice when it comes to working with a variable is that you can add any kind of value that you would like to it. The important part is that you make sure that you add in the equal sign between the value and the variable so the compiler knows what is supposed to go with what. In some cases, you will be able to add more than one value to a single variable, just by adding in more equal signs to the process, making things a little easier to work with depending on the code you want to work with.

6. The objects and the classes

One of the things that is going to distinguish the Python language apart from some of the other coding languages that are a bit older is that it operates using classes and objects that help you to keep it all organized and can make sure that the right parts show up at the right times within your code.

A programmer who is just getting started with this kind of coding is going to find it is easier to think about the objects and the classes like having a box with some items inside. Each of the boxes will be like the classes, and inside you will place certain objects that the class is meant to hold onto for organization. You can add in as many of these objects into a single class as you would like, and depending on your code, you can also have as many of these classes as you would like. However, the important thing to worry about is that when someone looks into some of your classes and understand why the objects are found inside the same class together.

You do not have to make all of the objects in the class identical, and you don' t want to make this your whole goal either. While these items don' t need to be identical, they do need to be related back to one another in some manner or another and it should make sense why the programmer added them into the same class. So, you can have a class that holds onto farm animals for example, or different types of vehicles.

The reason that Python is going to focus on the classes and objects is because this is a much better way for us to split up the information that we are using, and for us to make sure that we have stored it properly to find later. Unlike some of the other coding languages that are out there, Python ensures that the right parts of the code show up when you want them to.

As you can see, there are a lot of different parts that come together to help us work on a Python code. And when we learn how to work with all of these different parts, and understand how to write codes in this beneficial language, you will be able to put it to good use with some of the other libraries that can be added on in order to do all of your work with data science and data analysis in no time.

Chapter 8: Some of the Best Python Libraries to Help with Data Science

Python is one of the best coding languages that you are able to work with when you want to do some work with data science. But the regular library that comes installed with the Python language is not going to be able to handle all of the work that needs to be done with this field. This doesn' t mean that you are stuck though. There are many extensions and other libraries that work with Python, that can do some wonderful things when it comes to working on data science. When you are ready to start analyzing some of the data that you have been able to collect and learn some valuable insights out of them, here are some of the best coding libraries that work with Python as well.

NumPy and SciPy

The first part of the Python libraries for data science that we are going to take a look at is the NumPy, or Numeric and Scientific Computation, and the SciPy library. NumPy is going to be useful because it is going to help us lay down the basic premises that we need for scientific computing in Python. It is going to help us get ahold of functions that are precompiled and fast to help with numerical and mathematical routines as needed.

In addition to some of the benefits that we listed out above, NumPy is able to come in and optimize some of the programming that comes with Python by adding in some powerful structures for data. This makes it easier for us to efficiently compute matrices and arrays that are multi-dimensional.

Scientific Python, which is known as SciPy, is going to be linked together with NumPy, and it is often that you can' t have one without the other. When you have SciPy, you can lend a competitive edge to what happens with NumPy. This happens when you enhance some of the useful functions for minimization, regression, and more.

When you want to work with these two libraries, you need to go through the process of installing the NumPy library first and getting that all setup and ready to work with Python. From there, you can install the SciPy library and get to work with using the Python coding language with any of your goals or projects that include data science.

Pandas

The second type of Python library that we can use to help out with data science is going to be known as Pandas, or Python Data Analysis Library. The name of the library is going to be so important when it shows us how we can use this kind of library to help us get started.

Pandas is going to be a tool that is open-sourced and can provide us with data structures that are easy to use and high in performance and it comes with all of the tools that you need to complete a data analysis in the Python code. You can use this particular library to add in data structures and tools to complete that data analysis, no matter what kind you would like to do. Many industries like to work with this Python library for data science will include engineering, social science, statistics, and finance.

The best part about using this library is that it is adaptable, which helps us to get more work done. It also works with any kind of data that you were able to collect for it, including uncategorized, messy, unstructured, and incomplete data. Even once you have the data, this library is going to step in and help provide us with all of the tools that we need to slice, reshape, merge, and more all of the sets of data we have.

Pandas is going to come with a variety of features that makes it perfect for data science. Some of the best features that come with the Pandas library from Python will include:

1. You can use the Pandas library to help reshape the structures of your data.
2. You can use the Pandas library to label series, as well as tabular data, to help us see an automatic alignment of the data.

3. You can use the Pandas library to help with heterogeneous indexing of the data, and it is also useful when it comes to systematic labeling of the data as well.
4. You can use this library because it can hold onto the capabilities of identifying and then fixing any of the data that is missing.
5. This library provides us with the ability to load and then save data from more than one format.
6. You can easily take some of the data structures that come out of Python and NumPy and convert them into the objects that you need to Pandas objects.

Matplotlib

When you work on your data science, you want to make sure that after gathering and then analyzing all of the data that is available you also find a good way to present that information to others so they can gain all of the insights quickly. Working with visualizations of some sort, depending on the kind of data you are working with, can make it easier to see what information is gathered and how different parts are going to be combined together.

This is where the Matplotlib is going to come in handy. This is a 2D plotting library from Python, and it is going to be capable of helping us to produce publication-quality figures in a variety of formats. You can also see that it offers a variety of interactive environments across a lot of different platforms as well. This library can be used with the scripts form Python, the Python and the IPython shell, the Jupyter notebook, four graphical interface tool kits, and many servers for web applications.

The way that this library is going to be able to help us with data science is that it is able to generate a lot of the visualizations that we need to handle all of our data, and the results that we get out of the data. This library is able to help with generating scatterplots, error charts, bar charts, power spectra, histograms, and plots to name a few. If you need to have some kind of chart or graph to go along with your data analysis, make sure to check out what the matplotlib option can do for you.

Scikit-Learn

Scikit-Learn is going to be a module that works well in Python and can help with a lot of the state of the art algorithms that are found in machine learning. These algorithms that work the best with the Scikit-Learn library will work with medium-scale unsupervised and supervised machine learning problems so you have a lot of applications to make all of this work.

Out of the other libraries that we have talked about in this guidebook, the Scikit-Learn library is one of the best options from Python when it comes to machine learning. This package is going to focus on helping us to bring some more machine learning to non-specialists using a general-purpose high-level language. With this language, you will find that the primary emphasis is going to be on things like how easy it is to use, the performance, the documentation, and the consistency that shows up in the API.

Another benefit that comes with this library is that it has a minimal amount of dependencies and it is easy to distribute. You will find that this library shows up in many settings that are commercial or academic. Scikit-Learn is going to expose us to a consistent and concise kind of interface that can work with some of the most common algorithms that are part of machine learning, which makes it easier to add in some machine learning to the data science that you are working with.

Theano

Theano is another great library to work with during data science, and it is often seen as one of the highly-rated libraries to get this work done. In this library, you will get the benefit of defining, optimizing, and then evaluating many different types of mathematical expressions that come with multi-dimensional arrays in an efficient manner. This library is able to use lots of GPUs and perform symbolic differentiation in a more efficient manner.

Theano is a great library to learn how to use, but it does come with a learning curve that is pretty steep, especially for most of the people who have learned how to work with Python because declaring the variables and building up some of the functions that you want to work with will be quite a bit different from the premises that you learn in Python.

However, this doesn' t mean that the process is impossible. It just means that you need to take a bit longer to learn how to make this happen. With some good tutorials and examples, it is possible for someone who is brand new to Theano to get this coding all done. Many great libraries that come with Python, including Padas and NumPy, will be able to make this a bit easier as well.

TensorFlow

TensorFlow, one of the best Python libraries for data science, is a library that was released by Google Brain. It was written out mostly in the language of C++, but it is going to include some bindings in Python, so the performance is not something that you are going to need to worry about. One of the best features that come to this library is going to be some of the flexible architecture that is found in the mix, which is going to allow the programmer to deploy it with one or more GPUs or CPUs in a desktop, mobile, or server device, while using the same API the whole time.

Not many, if any, of the other libraries that we are using in this chapter, will be able to make this kind of claim. This library is also unique in that it was developed by the Google Brain project, and it is not used by many other programmers. However, you do need to spend a bit more time to learn the API compared to some of the other libraries. In just a few minutes, you will find that it is possible to work with this TensorFlow library in order to implement the design of your network, without having to fight through the API like you do with other options.

Keras

Keras is going to be an open-sourced library form Python that is able to help you to build up your own neural networks, at a high level of the interface. It is going to be pretty minimalistic, which makes it easier to work with, and the coding on this library is going to be simple and straightforward, while still adding in some of the high-level extensibility that you need. It is going to work either TensorFlow or Theano along with CNTK as the backend to make this work better. We can remember that the API that comes with Keras is designed for humans to use, rather than humans, which makes it easier to use and puts the experience of the user right in front.

Keras is going to follow what are known as the best practices when it comes to reducing the cognitive load. This Python library is going to offer a consistent and simple APIs to help minimize how many actions the user has to do for many of the common parts of the code, and it also helps to provide feedback that is actionable and clear if an error does show up.

In this library, we find that the model is going to be understood as a sequence, or it can be a graph of standalone, fully-configurable modules that you are able to put together with very few restrictions at the time. Neural layers, optimizers, activation functions, initialization schemes, cost functions, and regularization schemes are going to be examples of the standalone modules that are combined to create a new model. You will also find that Keras is going to make creating a new module simple, and existing module that are there can provide us with lots of examples to work with.

Caffe

The final Python library that we will take a look at in order to do some work with data science is going to be Caffe. This is a good machine learning library to work with when you want to focus your attention on computer vision. Programmers like to use this to create some deep neural networks that are able to recognize objects that are found in images and it has been explored to help recognize a visual style as well.

Caffe is able to offer us an integration that is seamless with GPU training and then is highly recommended any time that you would like to complete your training with some images. Although this library is going to be preferred for things like research and academics, it is going to have a lot of scope to help with models of training for production as well. The expressive architecture that comes with it is going to encourage application and innovation as well.

In this kind of library, you are going to find that the models will be optimized and then defined through configuration without hard coding in the process. You can even switch between the CPU and the GPU by setting a single flag to train on a GPU machine, and then go through and deploy to commodity clusters, or even to mobile devices.

These are just a few of the different libraries that you are able to use when it comes to working on Python, and they will ensure that you are going to see the best results any time that you want to explore a bit with data science. While the traditional form of the Python library, the one that comes with the original download, is not going to be able to handle some of the different parts that come with data science, you can easily download and add on these other Python libraries and see exactly what steps they can help with when it comes to gathering, cleaning, analyzing, and using the data that you have with data science.

Chapter 9: Terms to Know

Before we end this part of our journey on data science, it is important for us to spend some time learning about the different terms that are found in the world of data science. Some of these we have already been able to take some time to discuss, but others will be brand new. Learning all of these, and having a good understanding of each one is going to make a difference in how well you can understand and use data science and big data in your own business endeavors as well. Some of the terms that you should know that concern this industry will include:

1. **Business intelligence:** BI is going to be the process we use to analyze and then report historical data that is going to guide the decisions we make in the future. This can help leaders make better decisions moving forward, simply because it can determine what happened in the past using the data that is there.

2. **Data engineering:** Data engineers are going to be responsible for building the infrastructure through which data is gathered, cleaned, stored, and prepped so that the data scientist can then do their work. Good engineers are invaluable, and building a data team without these individuals can cause some issues down the line.

3. **Decision science:** Under the umbrella that we have of data science, the decision scientist is going to be able to apply technology and math to help solve business problems and add in behavioral science and some design thinking to help them provide the best products to the customer.

4. **Artificial intelligence:** Computer systems that have artificial intelligence on them are able to perform a variety of tasks that would normally require a human to do them. This doesn' t necessarily mean that the system has to replicate the mind of the human, but it is going to use the reasoning of humans as its own model to provide us with better services, or to create better products for the customer.

5. **Machine learning:** This is part of the category of artificial intelligence and it is going to refer to the process by which a system learns from the data that is added in, and then can identify some of the patterns that are in the data. These found patterns are then applied to some of the new requests and problems. This model is going to allow the data scientist to teach a computer the proper way to carry out a task, rather than having to take a step by step approach to programming.

6. **Cross-validation:** This is going to be a method that is used to help us validate the accuracy of the stability of the model we are using in machine learning. Although there are some different methods of cross-validation that you can use, the most basic out of these is going to involve splitting the training set into two, and then training one of these sets before applying it to the second one. Since you already know what output you should be getting here, it is a good way to test out the validity of the model as you go.

7. **Deep learning:** This is going to be a more advanced form of machine learning which is going to refer to a system that has multiple layers of outputs and inputs. In deep learning, it is required to have several rounds of data inputs and outputs to help the computer solve some of the real-world problems.

8. **A/B testing:** This is often a method that is used during the development of a product. This is going to be a type of randomized experiment in which you can test out two variants to determine the best course of action based on how the customer responded to it.

9. **Hypothesis testing:** This is a method that will use statistics in order to determine the probability that a given hypothesis is going to be true. This is something that we will see quite a bit in clinical research

10. **Statistical power:** This is going to simply be the probability of making a correct decision to reject the null hypothesis when this null hypothesis turns out to be false. To put this in other terms, it is the

likelihood that a study is going to detect an effect when there is no effect to find.

11. **The standard error:** This is going to be the measure of the accuracy, statistically, of an estimate. The larger the sample size that you work with, the lower the standard error that you will work with.

12. **Causal inference:** This is going to be a process that tests whether there is a relationship between the cause and the effect of a situation. This is something that becomes the goal in the health and social sciences. In these situations, we not only need some good algorithms and good data, but an expert in the subject matter can be important as well.

13. **Exploratory Data Analysis or EDA:** This is going to be one of the first steps that happen when analyzing a set of data. With the techniques that come with EDA, the data scientist is able to summarize the main characteristics of the set of data and then can inform some of the development of models that are more complex, or list out the next steps in the process that are the most logical.

14. **Data visualization:** This is going to be one of the key components that come with data science. They are basically the visual representations that we get when we take text-based information. This makes it easier to recognize some of the patterns, correlations, and trends that are found in all of that data. It is usually helpful to see how important or significant the data can be when it is placed in a visual context, rather than left in the text format.

15. **Data models:** These models are going to help us define how the sets of data are going to be connected to one another, and how they are processed and then stored inside our system. These models are going to show us the structure of the database, including the constraints and the relationships, which is going to be helpful in getting the data scientist to understand how you can best store any data that you bring in, while also manipulating the data.

16. **Data warehouse:** This data warehouse is going to be any kind of repository that the company wants to use. It is where all of the data a company collects

is going to be stored until it can be analyzed. The data warehouse is also going to be used as a type of guide to make some of the management decisions.

Part 2:

Putting it All to Work – Practical Examples to Work with Data Science

A List of Tables

Table 1: A Data Set of Classic Books

The first thing that we are going to work on is creating one of our own databases or datasets to hold onto some of our favorite books, or even to just make a list of books that we own in our home. This can even work when we want to run a book store and we need to be able to keep track of all the information that is there. The neat thing here is that we are able to create this kind of data set, and it is often easier than we may have thought in the beginning.

Databases are going to be used for a variety of activities, for everything from keeping track of the possessions in your home to tracking the thousands of employees who are in your business. But no matter what your plan is when it comes to using the database, the fundamental building blocks that come with the design of a database are going to be the same.

These databases are helpful because they are going to use tables to help store their information, and then each of these tables will contain a number of related fields. In the case of a database that will hold onto books, you have to make sure that there is enough information inside the table to identify the books and find what you need in a quick and efficient manner.

The first step that we need to use in order to create this database is to get onto the computer you would like to use and open up the program that you want to use to create the database. You can then click on the File menu and choose New from the options that are listed out. As you are in this part, click on the table for Tables, and then choose the option that lists "Create table in design view" out of those options. This design view is nice because it is going to give you a lot of flexibility when you are actually doing the building of the table, and entering the right fields into it.

At this point, we need to figure out what information is going to be unique to each record. In the case of making our own book database, we need to add in things like the name of the book, the genre, and the ISBN code to help make it easier to find. We will start out with the ISBN code as the first field. To do this, you can highlight the field that you are working on, right-click, and then select on the primary key. This is going to make the ISBN the index for the database, and can really make some of the searches you want to do faster. It will also ensure that when we are doing this, no new record can be added into the database without an ISBN present.

When the ISBN field is ready, you can enter in the remainder of the fields. This is going to depend on what you would like to have present as you work through all of this, but for a book database it could include things like the name of the author, the title, the publication date, and more. Anything to make it a bit easier for your customers and others to find the information they need on the book when doing a search

For the next step, we need to click on the menu for file and then choose save to make sure that the table gets saved. When you are doing the saving process, you need to give the table a name that is really descriptive to make it easier to pull up later. You could go with something like Books for now though.

When the file is saved and ready to go, it is time to click on the tab for Forms, and then choose the option that says "Create form by using wizard". This is just one of the options that you can use, but it is also the easiest way for you to create your own data entry form so we are going to stick with this one. When the form comes up, you can select your Books table and then click on any of the fields that you are interested in including. It is often a good idea if you are able to include in all of the fields that were present in the database as you work on making this kind of data entry form.

While you are in this step, you can make some selections about the form that you are working with. You can choose the appearance options that go with the form and when it is done to your liking, you can click on Finish to get the form completed. The form will then open up for you so that you can easily preview it. Enter the data into the form as you get to each new book. The data that you enter into this form will be able to save automatically for you into the underlying table, so you won' t have to do as much work here.

Table 2: Diabetes Study Data Set

The next part of this process that we are going to take a look at is the idea of diabetes and how this can be put into a data set as well. With this, we want to figure out how likely it is that someone is going to develop diabetes within a few years or more, based on how the model is set up. This one is also going to work with some historical data to make sure that all of the parts come together and make sense, and if the project is trained and tested right, it can be pretty accurate.

To make this set of data work, we need to be able to work with the historical data that is out there about patients who have been tested for diabetes, and if they have developed this disorder or not, and even if they already have this disorder. Getting these medical records will help us to make sure that we have the right information present, the information that can train the machine to know when someone has diabetes, and what signs and symptoms and other information they had at the same time.

So, for the training part, the data scientist may decide to gather up a set of data that includes patients who were diagnosed with diabetes, and a list of those who were not diagnosed with diabetes. There would also be other information about the patient such as where they worked, their age, their height and weight, how active they were, and more. This data, for both the patients with the disease and those without, would be fed not the model and used for the training and the testing part of the process.

When the model is set up with all of that information, it will then be able to accurately predict who is likely to get diabetes, based on how well they match up with the data that the model was presented. There are of course going to be those people who don' t fit the mold and may get diabetes even though they don' t match up, or may not get diabetes even though they do match up, so this model will not be accurate all of the time.

Even without 100 percent accuracy, it can help out doctors and other medical professionals determine who is at the highest risk when it comes to developing diabetes and even other serious diseases along the way. A good example of one of the data sets that you are able to work with diabetes and to see how well the model can predict whether or not someone will develop this disorder will include:

https://archive.ics.uci.edu/ml/datasets/Diabetes

Table 3: A Data Set of Emails: Spam or No Spam

At one point or another, we are all going to face the problem of having some spam show up in our email. Often the email that we are using is going to be set up in order to understand the difference between spam and non-spam emails, but there are times when some of the spam gets into the wrong box on the email. Learning how this process works, and how you are able to use it for your own needs can be important here to provide you with a process that works, and a good example of using the Python language.

The thing that we need to do here is to make sure that the email knows when a new message is spam, and when it is something that you will actually see. The email provider, as well as the algorithm that we are going to use, is able to take a look at millions of emails that have been labeled as either spam or non-spam. It can then learn some of the patterns and wording that show up in the emails that are labeled as spam, and can make sure these emails make it into your spam folder rather than into the inbox.

In the beginning, the email system will be accurate quite a bit, but there will be some spam that ends up in your inbox. As you click on the email and call it spam, and you work with that system, you will find that the algorithm learns, and the frequency of those spam emails ending up in your inbox will go down and down even more.

There are a few different algorithms that you are able to use to make this one happen. But for this particular option, you will find that working with the Naïve Bayes algorithm is going to be the most accurate option because it comes in with an accuracy of 98 percent.

There are going to be a few things that you need to have in place in order to work with the spam classification that happens with Naïve Bayes, and these will include:

1. You need to import the right libraries, including matplotlib, pandas, and NumPy.
2. You need to take the time to explore the set of data that you want to utilize.
3. You need to do the right kind of distribution of spam ad non-spam plots to make things happen.
4. You can work through an analysis of the text.
5. You can do the feature engineering.
6. Work with a predictive analysis which is going to include a multinomial Naïve Bayes.

You will be able to find the data set that is needed to work on this pam or no spam project with the help of the Python code at the following link: https://www.kaggle.com/ahkhalwai55/sms-spam-detection-with-deployment

A List of Illustrations

Figure 1: A Skills-Set Desideratum for a Data Science

To start with, data science is going to be a talent-based discipline with a lot of capabilities that come with it. Platforms, tools, and various infrastructures for IT are going to all come into it, but they play more of a secondary role in the process. Even with this being true, software and technology companies all around the world are going to spend a lot of money talking those in charge of a business to buy or license a product that is going to not provide all of the outcomes that are needed.

The reason that this ends up not being that satisfactory in the process is that it is not necessarily the software that you need to focus on. It is more about the talent of the person who is able to go through all of this data and find the information and insights that you need. But while this talent is important to the process, it is going to be rare and hard to find.

So, what is needed in order to perform some of the essential parts that come with data science. Each person who enters into this field is going to be different and have some specialties when it comes to what they are able to do with their talents and skills. But with this in mind, we also need to remember that there are a few skills that all of these professionals are going to share in common. Some of the skills that a data scientist needs to have in order to complete their job will include:

Education. A data scientist needs to have a good education in order to complete their job. It is estimated that about 91 percent of those in this field are going to hold a minimum of a Master' s degree, and almost half of them are going to have a PhD. There are some exceptions to this of course, but in most cases, if you would like to see success in this field, then you need to have a higher level of education in order to understand how the algorithms work, and what you are able to do with them.

Some coding experience. The next thing that a professional in this kind of field will need to have some understanding with is how to code. Python is one of the best languages to use when it comes to data science, and most of the professionals in this career choice will learn at least a little bit about Python. Other languages that work for data science will include Perl, C or C++, and Java. If you are just getting started with data science and want to be able to do some coding, then Python is going to be the best option.

In addition to working with the Python language, these professionals are going to need to spend some time with machine learning as well. The techniques that come with machine learning are quickly becoming an integral part of the job of a data scientist because many of the algorithms that come with this part of artificial intelligence can really make the work of a data scientist easier. If you want to transition into this kind of field, then working with machine learning is something that you must know how to do.

Next on the list is going to be data that is unstructured. It is critical for anyone who would like to be a data scientist to learn how to work with data that is not structured. This means that the data is going to be a bit messy, and probably will not have any labels that come with it. You are able to get this unstructured data from a variety of locations including audio, sensor data, video feeds, and even social media.

There are also going to be a few skills that are not technical that can fit in with this as well. For example, someone who wants to work in this field needs to have intellectual curiosity. This is a phrase that is popping up all over the place, especially when we are talking about how data scientists are doing their work. This is going to just mean that you need to have the curiosity that it takes to look through a lot of information, and figure out what is there and how it can help a business.

Business acumen is another important part that is going to sneak in here. To be a data scientist and also hold a role in business, you need to have a good amount of understanding in the industry that you want to work in. You also need to have a good understanding of some of the business problems that your company is looking to solve. There are always a lot of problems that need to be solved on a regular basis, but you have to pick out the one that is the most important and then focus on that instead.

And finally, someone who wants to work in the field of data science also needs to have some good communication skills in place. You can spend a lot of time going through the data and learning what is found in it, and how you can use that information. But if you are not able to properly communicate what information and insights you were able to find int hat information, then you just wasted a lot of time.

We have to remember that those who work with data science have a lot of technical knowledge, which is great.

But they may spend time showing the results to someone who doesn' t have a lot of technical knowledge. With the right kind of communication skills present, they may find that they are able to show their information and share it with others, without having a lot of confusion or having to go back and fix the results later on.

Figure 2: The DIKW Pyramid

We are going to take a look now at the DIKW Pyramid r model. This model is going to come under a few different names, but it stands for Data, Information, Knowledge, and Wisdom Model. This is going to be an important part of data science and is a graphical representation of how knowledge can be organized inside of your own company.

We already will start with the assumption that your company is going to collect data. And we know that any time we collect this data, it is in the raw form, and it is going to come in unorganized and jumbled. This DIKW model is going to help describe how we can take that data and then process and transform it into information, knowledge, and wisdom that we can use to propel our business forward.

This model of handling the data and turning it into wisdom is something that we are able to view using two different angles, the understanding and the contextual. As per the contextual concept, one is going to move from a phase of gathering the parts of data that they need, the connection that they need to make from the various parts of the raw data which is the information, then they can form new and meaningful contents out of it, which is the knowledge. Then this all comes together and we can conceptualize and join those whole and meaningful contents, which is going to be the wisdom.

From the perspective of understanding, this kind of pyramid is going to be seen as a process that starts out with research, and then we absorb, do, interact, and reflect on all of that information the way that we need to.

It is possible to take this kind of model and go a bit further by representing it through the terms of time. For example, the data, the information, and then the knowledge levels are going to be something that we are able to see in the past, because they were things that we accomplished in the past. And then the final step, which is the wisdom, is going to help represent the future that we will work with and how we can handle all of the data that we bring in.

The first step that comes with this model is going to be the data. Collecting all of the raw data is going to be the primary requirement that comes with reaching a meaningful result that you are able to use in the end. Any of the records, the tracking, the logging, and the measurements that you can use is going to be considered data that can be used to make decisions. Since the raw data is going to be collected in bulk, it is going to include some contents that are useful, and some that are not. The data that we are talking about in this section is raw data, data that we have not been able to sort through yet, and that is what the other steps are all about.

Once we have collected all of the data, it is time to move on to the information part of the pyramid. This information is going to be the data that has been given meaning by defining some of the relational connections. The word "meaning" will be the processed and understandable data that could be useful for the company, but sometimes there is still some that you are not able to work with. In the information processing system, the relational database is going to create information from the data that we store inside. The information stage here is going to be important because it helps to reveal the relationships that are in the data, and then the analysis is going to be carried out so we can find out all of the answers that are there. You can think of this like the stage where we find the who, what, when, and where questions.

The third stage is going to be the knowledge stage. This is going to mean the appropriate collection of information that we can make into something useful. The knowledge stage of this hierarchy is going to be a process that is more deterministic. When someone is able to memorize information based on the usefulness, then they are said to have accumulated knowledge. Every piece of knowledge on its own is going to have a meaning that is useful, but it is not going to be able to generate some more knowledge on its own.

And then there is wisdom. This is going to be the process that we take to get to the final result in the process by calculating through the extrapolation of the knowledge. It is going to consider the output from all of the other levels of the model, and will process them through some special types of human programming, including the ethical codes and the moral codes.

This is why it is a good thing to consider wisdom as the thought as the process by which you can make a decision between the right and the wrong, the good and the bad or any decisions of improvement. We can also say that in this stage, the knowledge found in the other stage is applied and implemented in our practical life. This wisdom is going to be the highest level of the pyramid, and it is responsible for helping us to find answers to any of the questions of Why that we have.

All four of these stages need to come into play when it comes to handling all of the raw data that your company is taking in already. Being able to keep all of them organized and ensuring that you sort through them in the proper manner will make a big difference on not only the type of data that you are able to look over, but even on the information that you are able to glean out of that data in the first place.

Figure 3: Data Science Pyramid

In this section, we are going to spend some time looking at the pyramid that can be used in data science to make sure that we can fully gather and understand the data that has been collected. This will ensure that we are going to see the best results possible, and that we can really understand it and use it to make smarter decisions overall. Let' s dig in and see what the data science pyramid is all about and what the different parts is that go along with this pyramid.

The data science pyramid is going to start out with a question. This is seen by many professionals to be the hardest part of starting a new project because you have to think about the right question, and make it specific enough, to figure out what is in the data. This helps you to set the right parameters, and ensures that you will actually be able to find the information that you need.

We should never go blindly into the process of analyzing our data first, we need to ask some kind of question about the data. We may not even need to have the data on hand when we ask the question, and we can use the question to help lead us in the right direction for finding the data. After we have asked our question, it is time to move into the data science pyramid and look at some of the other parts of analyzing our data.

1. Data selection and gathering

After the question has been asked, it is time to actually go out there and select and gather the data we want. We have to think about the type of data that we would like to gather for our question at hand. This is going to be the most important step because the parameters that we choose for the data will be what we should stick with until the end, or we have to restart from the beginning if we want to change things up.

The final results that we get here are going to be completely dependent on only these parameters of the data, and nothing else. Here we might be gathering some data from a lot of different sources, and all of them will bring us data in a variety of formats. We may even see that they contain data that has been organized in a variety of manners as well.

2. Cleaning the data and storing it

These two tiers are going to come together in many cases as you collect the data. Be aware that they often take up a good amount of the time you spend on these projects as well based on how much data you use, and how many different sources you gather the data from. For this step, we need to be able to design a database where we can store all of the data that we gather. We also need to have a good management system for the database to ensure it can handle the kind of data that we are going to bring in.

The data that we have gathered needs to be cleaned for such things as inaccurate, missing, and corrupt entries. Then, the data that we bring in from a variety of sources has to be integrated with one another to form a cohesive set of data. This is where the storage is going to come in because a schema has to be chosen so that all of the data we have gathered from different sources can be readily formatted to go into the database

3. Feature extraction

This tier is going to be where we work to reduce the data down to just some of the parts that we really need to work with. We want to make sure that the data we are working with is easy to handle. The main goal that we see is going to be to combine or consolidate the variables into chunks that are easier to look over, shrinking them as much as possible to help out here

When we work with this step, we could use a lot of different techniques to help us lower and limit the amount of data we have. Keep in mind that there are some cases where we are not able to reduce the data as much as we would like, and this means we have to leave the variables where they are. But these different methods will ensure that you can reduce the information as much as possible.

4. Extracting the knowledge

This is the tier that a lot of companies are excited to get to. This is where you are going to be able to answer that question from the beginning. With the data already formatted in a nice manner, and the right features selected, it is now time to apply the analysis that you need the one that is the most appropriate for your data, be it a machine learning algorithm, regression, a time series analysis, and more.

You have to pick out the right method that will help you to go through all of that data and find out what knowledge is there. The type of question that you asked in the beginning, and the type of data that you have to look through will help determine what algorithm or method you would like to work with, but it is possible that you will need to add in a few at a time to find the one that is the best.

5. Visualization

Once you know the information that you want to work with, and you have been able to answer the question that you asked in the beginning, it is time to take this a bit further and actually turn the information into visualization. This will include something like a chart or a graph to help you understand what information is inside. This helps us to see what is inside the information in an easy to read format, rather than trying to sift through all of the data and numbers and do it for ourselves. You should make a visualization to go with this process to ensure that you and others who need to know about all of that information at a glance.

Figure 4: The CRISP-DM Life Cycle

CRISP-DM, is going to stand for Cross-Industry Standard Process for Data Mining. It is going to be an industry-proven way to guide the efforts that you do with data mining. As a methodology, it is going to include some of the descriptions of the typical phases of a project, the tasks that are involved with all of the phases, and an explanation of the various relationships that are going to come with all of these tasks. It can also be a process type of model, and when this happens, it is going to provide us a good overview of the life cycle of data mining.

The model of the life cycle is going to consist of six different phases that have arrows present to indicate the dependencies that are the most important and frequent between the various phases. The sequence of the phases is not strict. In fact, most of the projects are going to go back and forth between the phases when it is necessary.

The nice thing about this kind of model is that it is flexible to your needs, and you are able to add in the customizations that you need pretty easily. For example, if your aim in the company is to detect when money laundering is happening, it is likely that you will go through and sift a large amount of data, without having a specific goal for the modeling in place.

For this example, instead of modeling, your work is going to spend some time focusing on the data exploration and the visualization that you can work with in order to find any of the patterns that are suspicious in financial data. This model is helpful because it can allow you to create a model of data mining that are not strict and stuck in one place, but that is going to be able to fit some of your own particular needs.

In this kind of situation, the modeling, evaluation, and deployment phases might be less relevant compared to understanding the data or the phase for preparing the data. However, it is always important for us to consider the variety of questions that can be raised during these later phases for our long term planning and some of the goals that we have in the future when it comes to mining the data at hand.

Figure 5: A Typical Small Data and Big Data Architecture for Data Science

When you want to create your very own architecture for either small data or big data, there are going to be a few layers that come into play. These are going to include the data sources the ingestion strategy of the data, the data storage, the data processing, and the data consumption. We are going to take some time to quickly look at all five of these to see how we can use them to create a useful architecture for all kinds of data, and to ensure that we are able to glean some of the most important parts out of it all.

Get to the source

The first part of this architecture is going to be identifying the sources for our data. This is so important because it helps us to find all of the different source systems and then we can categorize them based on their type and their nature. Some of the different points that we need to consider when we are profiling the sources of data will include:

1. We need to be able to identify some of the external and the internal sources systems.
2. We need to do a high-level assumption for the amount of data that we are able to ingest from all of the sources.
3. We can take some time to identify the mechanisms that are used in order to get the data. This means we figure out if it is a push or a pull kind of system.
4. We need to then determine the type of data source we are using. This would include figuring out if it is a stream, a web service, a file, or a database.
5. We can then determine the data type that we are working with including unstructured, semi-structured and structured.

The ingestion strategy and acquisition

We need to know how we plan to get the data and look through it. This is going to be done with the process of extract, load, and transform, in that order. Some of the points that we need to take a look at when it comes to this particular stage will include:

1. We need to determine how often we would like to ingest the data from each source we are using.
2. We need to consider whether there is a need to change up the semantics of the data and if we need to replace it.
3. We need to consider if there is any data validation, or any data transformation, required before we do ingest. This is something known as pre-processing.
4. We need to be able to segregate the source of data that are used based on the model that we plan to ingest them. This can be done in real-time, or in batches

Storage

A data scientist needs to be able to store a large amount of data of any kind that they want, and they should have the ability to scale it on a needed basis. We also need to consider the amount of IOPS, or input-output operations per second, that the process is able to provide to us. These are all important when determining the kind of storage that you would like to use with the data you are collecting. Each one is going to be important, and can help us to really hold onto the data and bring it out when needed.

Due to the fact that this storage is becoming easier to use, and less expensive, all of the time, it is easier than ever for companies to hold onto as much big data as they need, to bring it out later and really make some good analysis of that information. Now that you don't have to pick and choose as much as before, and can collect any of the data that you would like, it becomes a lot easier for you to find some of the best insights that come with the data you are working with.

There are going to be two types of analytical requirements that we have to consider when we are looking for storage. We want the storage to support some of the following:

1. Synchronous: This is when the data we store is analyzed in near real-time or real-time. If we go with this one, the storage that we are using needs to be optimized for low latency.
2. Asynchronous: This is when the data is captured, recorded, and then analyzed out in a batch

There are also a few different things that we need to consider and keep in mind when it comes to planning out some of the methodology that we want to use for storing our data, and these include:

1. The type of data that we are storing, whether it is incremental or historical.
2. The format of the data. We have to consider whether the data is unstructured, semi-structured, or structured.
3. The requirements for compression.
4. The frequency of the incoming data.
5. The pattern of query of the data
6. The consumers of the data.

The processing time

We also have to take a look at the processing that we can do with our data. The processing power that we have with our storage and with some of the different machine learning algorithms can make it easier for us to get a good idea of what is found in the data. The processing methodology that we use when it comes to handling all of that data you have is going to be driven by the requirements of the business. There are also a few methodologies that you can choose and they will include:

1. Batch processing: The Batch processing is going to be when we collect the input for a specific amount of time and then we run some transformations on it in a way that is more scheduled. This is going to usually handle historical data.

2. Real-time processing: This is where we will run all of the necessary transformations on the data right when the data is added into the system, usually when it is acquired.

3. Hybrid processing: This is going to be a combination of both the real-time and the batch processing needs.

The consumption

This final step is going to be all about the output that is provided when we get to the layer of processing. Different users, like the vendor, the partners, business users and administrator are going to consume the data that you find in a different format. The output of our analysis can be consumed by a recommendation engine or a business process and we can use this to improve our business as well. Some of the options that we can use when it comes to consuming the data we have will include:

1. Export datasets: There can be requirements for third party dataset generation.
2. Reporting and visualizations.
3. Data exploration
4. Adhoc querying.

Figure 6: The Traditional Process or Building Predictive Models and Scoring Data

Creating a predictive model is going to be important when it comes to working through some of the data that is present in your business. You are already collecting a large amount of data, so it makes sense that we want to be able to work on creating a model that is able to take that data and make some predictions based on what is going to happen with that data in the future. A successful project that works with predictive analytics is one that is executed on a step by step basis. Some of the major parts that come with the process of building our very own predictive model, and making some predictions that influence your business decisions will include:

Defining the business objects. The project that you do here has to start out with a business objective that you have been able to define well. The model is meant to address the question your business has. Clearly stating that the objective is going to allow you to define the scope of your projects, and then will make sure that you gather the right information from the start, and that you will use the right test to make sure that the project is successful.

From here, we need to be able to prepare the data. You are going to use all of that data you brought in to help train the model. The data is often found in a lot of different sources when you gather it, which means that we need to complete the preparation and cleansing process to make it work. Data can often come in messy, with outliers and lots of duplicate records, and can sometimes have missing values as well.

As you are working through your model, you want to make sure that the information that you have is as high quality as possible. The better the data you are using, the better the model will be as you work with it. Taking some time to do the training process is going to help us to get a lot of good results, and can make it easier to know our model is doing well.

Now we need to move on to sampling the data you will need to take the data that you have already collected and split it up into two different sets. These will include a set for training and a set for testing. You need to build up the model you choose with the set of data for training. Then, when all of the training is done, you can work with the test data to see if the output of the model is as accurate as possible.

Doing this is important and it is not something that you should skip out with. It is possible that with a limited set of data to train the data that you end up overfitting the model, which means that it is going to pick out some of the wrong characteristics as their output. A test set of data is going to be one of the best methods you can use in order to measure out the performance of the model you are working with.

With all of this in place, it is time to work with building up a model. Sometimes the data or the objectives of the business are going to help you figure out the right model or algorithm that you want to work with. Other times the approach that you should use is not going to be as easy to understand as you would like. You may need to explore the data and try out a few different algorithms to see which one will work the best. You can then use this experiment to pick out a good algorithm, and build up the model that you want to use with this information.

And finally, after all of the other work done and the model built up with the right algorithm, it is time to deploy the model and use it. You have to actually deploy your model in order to reap all of the benefits from it. This process can sometimes be done in one area, and other times you will need to coordination with other departments.

Your aim here is to build up a model that is deployable, and then come up with a method where you can show off this information to your stakeholders and make sure that everyone understands what is going on, and where all of the parts fit together as well.

Figure 7: A Simple Neural Network

We spent some time in this guidebook talking about how to work with the Python coding language in order to create some great codes and to make sure that we were able to do quite a bit with data science. Now it is time to take a look at some of the options that you can do, and one of the best places to start is with a simple neural network.

A neural network is going to be great to work with because the algorithms that come with it are designed in order to work similar to what we will see with the brain. It is meant to learn from past experiences, and form stronger connections when it is able to do something correctly. This process is also going to be able to work in order to learn from the mistakes that it has made so that it avoids those in the future.

This is a great process to work with when it comes to unsupervised machine learning, and getting it organized and ready to go is easier than you may think. This neural network, at least in the simple form, will help us to really organize our work, and can get a ton of information out of the data that we collected.

There are a lot of times when you will be able to work with a neural network, and some of these are going to be harder to handle than others. But we are going to spend a moment looking at the basic code that you can work with when using the Python language and writing out our own simple neural network. You can certainly expand this out to do some training and some testing, but a simple code that can be used to create one of these neural networks, just to see how it works without all of the extras, will include:

```
from numpy import exp, array, random, dot
training_set_inputs = array([[0, 0, 1], [1, 1, 1], [1, 0, 1], [0, 1, 1]]) training_set_outputs = array([[0, 1, 1, 0]]).T
random.seed(1)
synaptic_weights = 2 * random.random((3, 1)) - 1
for iteration in xrange(10000):
```

```
        output = 1 / (1 + exp(-(dot(training_set_inputs,
        synaptic_weights))))) synaptic_weights += 
        dot(training_set_inputs.T, (training_set_outputs -
        output) * output * (1 - output))
print 1 / (1 + exp(-(dot(array([1, 0, 0]),
synaptic_weights))))
```

Figure 8: A Deep Neural Network

A deep neural network is going to take some of the information that we talked about earlier and takes it a bit further. It recognizes that there is sometimes a need for deep learning in the work that we do, and can help us to really get some great programs done with machine learning.

While there are a variety of algorithms that you are able to use when it comes to artificial intelligence, these deep neural networks are going to be there to help out more with deep learning. In the brain, the most basic unit is going to be found in the neurons. But in a neural network, we are going to get this work done with signal processing, and then the mesh network that we create will connect it all. And as you can imagine with this process, all of the network can grow large over time.

A computer that has designed a neural network is going to have the programmer teach it to do a task by having to look at a lot of training examples, and then the network is going to come in and analyze that information. This information has gone through the process of having labels put on it ahead of time. a good example of how this works is when a neural network is presented with many objects that come in at one type, and then the computer, thanks to the analysis that it works on, will be able to see what patterns seem to show up over and over again. This helps the neural network to learn and remember this information to use at a later time.

With this in mind, we need to take some time to look at how the neural networks are going to learn. Unlike some of the other machine learning algorithms that are out there, neural networks, with the help of the deep leaning they can do, can' t be programmed in a direct manner for that task. Instead, they are going to have some requirements, just like how the developing brain of a child does that they have to be able to learn the information.

When you are teaching a child, you can' t just put some information in and have the child know everything. They have to go through the process and actually learn something for it to stick around. When they do this, then the information is going to stay there, and they can learn more and more along the way. The neural network is going to be the same. The algorithm has to be given a chance to learn along the way.

There are going to be two different methods that can be used to help the neural network learn the way that it should. These should include:

1. **Supervised learning.** This is one of the simplest learning strategies that are available as there is going to be labeled set of data. The computer can go through this, and then the algorithm is going to be modified in a manner until it is able to process the set of data needed to get the right results.

2. **Unsupervised learning.** This is going to be a different strategy that is going to be used when you do not have an available set of data already

labeled for the program to learn from. The neural network can come in here and analyze the set of data, and then the cost function can tell the network how close or far from the target it was. With this information, the neural network is going to make the right adjustments in order to increase how accurate it is.

3. **Reinforced learning.** When the neural network uses this kind of algorithm, it is going to be reinforced for any of the positive results, as it receives punishment for any of the results that are negative. These positive and negative results help the neural network to learn how they should behave over time.

There are a lot of uses and applications when it comes to these neural networks. For example, you could use the neural network to help with recognizing some handwriting of different people. While a human would have a better chance looking through the handwriting examples and seeing that they are at least different from one another, this is something that we need to be able to train the program to do.

To make sure that our computer is going to be able to learn how to recognize handwriting samples, and other complex tasks like this, the algorithm of neural networks can come into play. With some of the data science libraries for Python that we talked about earlier in this guidebook, you will be able to pull out the right algorithm to get all of this to work for you.

There are many tasks that can be done with the help of a neural network, and learning how to work with this process and how to write some of these, using some of the examples that we talked about earlier can make it that you can combine machine learning, Python, and data science all in one to get your project done.

These neural networks can even be used to help with some of the projects that you want to do with data science. You can even set up a network so that it can handle all of the data that we work with even on a continuous basis to keep track of everything. The network would be able to learn from the information that you present to it and will get better at making predictions as time goes on, providing a lot of benefits to the business that uses it.

Conclusion

Thank you for making it through to the end of *Python for Data Science*, let's hope it was informative and able to provide you with all of the tools you need to achieve your goals whatever they may be.

The next step is to start putting some of the information that we have discussed in this guidebook to good use. As a business, if you have not already started to collect data from various sources whether online, social media, from the customers who shop on your site or more, then you are already falling behind. It is only once that information is collected that you can begin the real work of sorting through all of that data and figuring out some of the information that is hidden inside. This guidebook spent some time looking at this process, and all of the steps that you can take to make data science, with the help of the Python coding language, work for you.

This guidebook has provided us with a lot of different information on data science, on how it works machine learning, the Python language, and even some of the examples of how you can put all of this together and actually make it all work. Often data science sounds difficult and too hard to work on, but this guidebook has shown us some of the practical steps that we can take to put it all together.

When you are finally ready to take on some of the data that you have been accumulating and you are excited to make this all work for you in terms of providing better customer service, and really seeing some good results in the decisions that you make for your business, make sure to check out this guidebook to help you get started with Python for data science.

Finally, if you found this book useful in any way, a review on Amazon is always appreciated!

www.ingramcontent.com/pod-product-compliance
Lightning Source LLC
Chambersburg PA
CBHW071126050326
40690CB00008B/1356